AND YOU SHALL
BE FREE

Deanna Langworthy

ISBN 979-8-88616-172-4 (paperback)
ISBN 979-8-88616-173-1 (digital)

Christian Faith Publishing
832 Park Avenue
Meadville, PA 16335
www.christianfaithpublishing.com

Printed in the United States of America

This book is dedicated to my Dad and my Uncle Dale Hammen. My Dad and I had a love-hate relationship. Throughout my childhood and into my thirties, my father was an alcoholic. I say "father" because he didn't become my Dad until he was paralyzed and became sober. At that point, by the grace of God, we were able to truly work through all that had happened. Both of us accepted responsibility for our part, sought forgiveness, and extended forgiveness. He became my Dad, my confidant, my partner in shenanigans, and a father figure to my children. Our restored relationship gave me the first glimpse that God may have more for me. I love you, Dad. I miss you, and I cannot wait to dance with you again in heaven one day.

My Uncle Dale showed me the love of a Dad when my own father was unable to. Uncle Dale loved like Jesus, and I truly believe his love allowed my heart to remain pliable for when God intervened, and all the healing transpired between me and my Dad. For that, and so much more, I will be eternally grateful. I know the two of you are hanging out together now in heaven, and I look forward to the day we will all be together again.

CONTENTS

WARNING

Some readers may find the recounting of my rape in chap-ter 8 offensive. The good Lord knows the rape offended me. However, it is integral to the processing of my rape, and the story would not be complete nor would the integrity of the book be intact without it. I hope the reader will accept it in the spirit in which it is offered.

ACKNOWLEDGMENTS

First, I want to thank my kids, Quinn and Isaiah. You had to grow up under the care of a traumatized mama—it had to have been so hard! If there are any regrets (and there are many), it is the effect my trauma had on you. Even though you both knew I loved you with all my heart, living with me had to be quite confusing at times. I'm sorry for any pain it caused you. By the grace of God, you both have grown up to be amazing men, and I am so thankful for that. I value the relationship I have with each of you so much and pray continually that God would bless you and continue to draw you closer to Him all the days of your lives.

Second, I want to thank my sister. Yes, I purposely don't identify which one; she knows who she is, and that is all that is important. God used our restored relationship to give me the courage to believe I truly could tackle the larger areas of trauma in my life. Your acknowledgment of the situation and apology was one of the most powerful and profound steps in my healing. Your love and friendship are invaluable to me, and I can't wait to see all God has in store for us as we finish this race God has for us on this earth. I love you.

Next, I want to thank my editor, Deanne McCarrison. Your encouragement to write a second book gave me the confirmation and push that I needed. Your patience and generosity know no end. Your belief in this project was a true blessing from God that at times sustained me in this process. Throughout our journey, you have become so much more than an editor; you are my lifelong friend.

Finally, to my Lord and Savior, Jesus Christ: When I think of all You have rescued and healed me from, my heart almost bursts in gratitude. I pray that You will use this book to bring healing to others who don't yet realize that **You** are the answer to their healing. I give all credit for this book to **You**. I give all glory and praise to **You,** and I thank you.

All my love,
Deanna

INTRODUCTION

As Jonah learned, if God is taking you to
Nineveh, then that's where you are going. Take
a boat or take a fish, the easy way or the hard
way, God will accomplish His purposes.
—Chuck Smith, Calvary Chapel Costa Mesa

Upon receiving my book *Grace and Peace* back from my editor, she said, "I believe there is a second book from this that God wants you to write." My heart sank. "I know," I replied. "He has been telling me the same thing." You see, God had shown me and let me experience His peace, but in that revelation, He had also given me a taste of something else—freedom. And freedom always comes at a cost. This is my story.

CHAPTER 1

Peel Your Onion

Freedom is somewhat of an oxymoron. Although it may be given freely, it almost always requires some type of work; at a minimum, the willingness to accept the gift if completely free. But in most cases, you need to agree to be an active participant in doing whatever needs to be done to achieve your freedom. In this case, the freedom being offered was big. God wanted me to be free from all the entanglements of my past, and there were many.

Over the course of our lives, we all develop many layers that make up our stories. These layers make up the entirety of all our joys, sorrows, losses, and gains. And like an onion, it can take many layers of "peeling" before we get to our core.

Now, I absolutely believe that God can do anything. There are times when a person is prayed over, God does a mighty work, and the recipient is instantly healed and set free. We see many examples of this in the Bible. But I also recognize that there are many times in life when the needed freedom isn't immediate. In these instances, I believe God wants us to be active participants in the freedom walk—to follow Him and, more importantly, to **trust** Him. If you are anything like me, the following isn't nearly as hard as trusting.

When I finished writing my first book, *Grace and Peace*, I was in a good place. I had just done something I didn't think was possible—I had written a book! Because I had never wanted to write the book, I literally went into the process kicking and fighting all the way. But God was faithful to His calling, and it was completed. The peace He had given me was like a drug, and I just couldn't get enough of it. Toward the end of writing the book, and even with no job, I literally felt as though worries just slid off me like water off a duck's back. And even though I was loving my peace-filled life, I also knew I had to have a job. It was January 2018, and I knew God had a job for me. My part was to have a mindset open to finding and taking it.

As I continued to both apply for jobs and talk to my recruiter, my prayer never changed. "Lord, please close every door except the one You want me to walk through; otherwise, I might mess up and choose the wrong one!" Not only did I pray this, but I had my family and friends praying the same thing. I knew that if I stayed in His will, I would be okay.

And then it happened. I was called in to interview for two different jobs. Job One was a full-time job with great benefits. The interview went very well, and I was immediately scheduled for a second. It seemed perfect! The location was in close proximity to my home, the benefits were phenomenal, and the woman who would be my boss seemed great. The second interview with the rest of the team was scheduled for the next week. I was excited. I found myself really hoping this was the job for me.

At about this time, the interview for Job Two was scheduled. It, too, would be for the following week. This job would be a short-term consulting job with no benefits but good pay. My excitement level about it was not comparable to what I felt about Job One, but I was very much trying to keep an open mind.

The second interview for Job One happened first. Meeting the team was everything I had hoped it would be. They seemed to really like me, and I really liked them. As I left, I was told it went very well and to expect a call soon. I was ecstatic and relieved! I knew this was my job but still went to the interview for Job Two later that week. It, too, went very well, and I was surprised by how interested I was in the opportunity. I knew I really needed to be in prayer about the opportunities, but I was still very much drawn to Job One.

Within a few days, I was in the exact dilemma I had prayed to avoid. Both companies had called with a verbal offer! Now, you would think that because I hadn't been working for five months that I would be ecstatic. I was happy, but I really wanted to be in God's will, and I had really hoped to not be in the place where I had to decide what that was. So I did what I knew—I prayed.

I prayed for wisdom. I prayed for discernment. I prayed for His will, not mine, to be done. Full disclosure, I **really** wanted that full-time job with benefits. After all, the consulting job was only for twelve weeks. That meant I could be in the exact same boat within three months. On the surface, this seemed like a no-brainer decision. Yet every time I prayed, I felt like He was telling me to take the consulting job. The more I prayed, the stronger the feeling got. I thought, *Ugh! This makes no sense! Who in their right mind would pass up a full-time job with benefits to take a twelve-week contract with no benefits?* Finally, while in prayer one day, I heard God whisper, "Who is your provider? Do you trust Me?" A feeling of conviction and shame overwhelmed me. I knew positively that this was a faith test, and I was failing. I needed to stop trying to change God's mind. I had a decision to make, and it was time to make it. Was I going to take the job that made sense to my mind or trust what God was telling me to do in my spirit? Would I choose to step out in faith and trust God for my provision? Or would I go back to my old ways and rely on myself?

There was no contest. Before I could be further tempted, I called the recruiter for Job One. I very politely declined the job, saying I had received another offer that I was taking. Then I quickly called the recruiter for Job Two and accepted the twelve-week consulting assignment. Even though this seemed like the craziest move ever, I knew deep in my heart and soul that I was doing the right thing. At the same time, I knew nobody else would agree, and I was okay with that too. God had a plan, and I was ready to see what it was.

I started my consulting job the next week. When I showed up, there were no supplies—no phone, no computer, no pens, nothing. And my "office" was the storage room! I had to laugh, or I probably would have cried. God certainly had a sense of humor, and He was definitely testing me. On a positive note, even though the setup was odd at best, I really seemed to have an instant soft spot for the people. I could tell from the start that this was not going to be like any job I had previously had, and that was okay. Again, I knew God had a plan. In His timing, it would be revealed.

It wasn't too long before that happened. The following week, I received a call from the recruiter about the job I had turned down. She had called to tell me I had made the right decision in turning down their verbal offer because just days after I had declined the job, it was announced that the company had been bought. If I had accepted that job, she would have been calling to rescind the offer because all open jobs had been closed so that the company could restructure. She went on to say that she really liked me and just wanted me to know I had made the right decision.

I couldn't believe my ears! So many thoughts were racing through my mind during the call. I thanked her and hung up the phone in disbelief. First off, who gets a call back from a recruiter after declining an offer with an update on what had happened with a job they declined? I had been in Human Resources for over twenty years and had never once done that unless I was trying to re-recruit someone. Second, what had God just done? My mind was blown as I realized that what had seemed foolish (taking the contract job instead of the full-time job with benefits) ended up being the decision that led to employment. True to His word, God had indeed provided. And again, I remembered that God's ways are not our ways, but His ways are always best.

The first couple of months flew by. I liked my boss and the employees, and there was plenty of work to be done. As a matter of fact, after explaining the workload to the boss, he immediately extended my contract for another three months. My twelve-week contract had turned into six months of employment. God was faithful.

You would think that I would have been soaring around on cloud nine with all of this answered prayer. After all, my book was in the process of being edited, and I was gainfully employed—what more could I want?

After some reflection, I realized that what was missing in my current situation was peace. Somewhere along the way, I had started to lose my peace again. I thought, *Seriously? I just finished writing a book titled* Grace and Peace, *and within a month of sending it to my editor, I am struggling with peace again? How can this be? What kind of a hypocrite am I?*

This was when God started to reveal His greater plan for me. He knows me, *every single layer.* He didn't want a shallow relationship with a happy glazing of peace on top, or even a mediocre relationship. He wanted to go deep— deeper than I had ever allowed—all the way to the core. And this would lead to more freedom than I had ever experienced. But first, things had to get real, and that level of "real" meant transparency like I had never agreed to previously. Doors would need to be widely opened that I had not only slammed shut but also boarded up to never be opened again. Oh yes, things were about to get real.

Transparency

How many of us are truly brave enough to be completely transparent regarding our past and who we truly are? The Bible tells us, "Don't copy the behavior and customs of this world, but let God transform you into a new person by changing the way you think. Then you will know what God wants you to do, and you will know how good and pleasing and perfect His will really is" (Romans 12:2 NLT). But the world does not chant this same mantra. No, the world says that only the beautiful—might I even suggest, the perfect—is fit to be shared. From the airbrushed, filtered photographs of models to the perfectly-staged photos on social media, much communication is an illusion. But what is real?

We've all done it—tried to come off as something we are not. Whether it's due to a lack of skill or lack of self-confidence, many times we "Fake it till we make it." The problem is that whenever people do this, they cease to be authentic. What may have started out as a lack of skills or confidence, or even a cover-up of past mistakes, can quickly turn into a lack of integrity due to the false charade. And the very worst thing is when you start to believe your own version of the story. God knows our truth. Even if we start to fool ourselves, we can never fool Him. No matter what we think, feel, or go through, our heart and soul are always transparent to Him—He knows all.

Yet sometimes we mistakenly believe that if we refuse to think or talk about the past, we can make it go away. And the uglier the thing that haunts our past is, the more likely we have shoved it deeper down into the "Do not go there" category. So we move on with our lives. We may even fool ourselves into believing that we "got over it." But in reality, what most have actually learned is to just push whatever "it" is down even deeper.

So how do you know? How do you know if the hurt or trauma from your past has really been resolved or if it is holding you in bondage? Rip off the Band-Aid. Ask yourself these questions:

1. Are there occurrences in your past that you are uncomfortable talking about, or even refuse to talk about?
2. If you are willing to talk about them, do you find yourself making excuses to justify or rationalize your past activities?
3. When talking about them, do you feel bitterness, anger, or even rage welling up inside of you?
4. Do you struggle to trust others because of events in your past?

5. Do you have a fear of and/or anger from something in your past that makes you unable to go there emotionally or verbally?

If you answered any of these questions with a yes, I would challenge that you are being held hostage by an occurrence, or occurrences, from your past that is (are) not allowing you to live your life to its fullest freedom. The first step toward fixing this is to be completely honest and transparent with yourself. Jesus said, "And you will know the truth, and the truth will set you free" (John 8:32). He is ready to help us. We just need to be willing to let Him.

* * * * *

Back in 2018, as I lay in bed trying to go to sleep, I started mentally beating myself up again. As my peace continued to roller-coaster, I couldn't get over feeling like a hypocrite. Just as Jacob wrestled with God in the book of Genesis, I, too, was determined to bring my grievance before God until I understood what was going on. I started praying. I poured out my heart. I shared how I didn't understand why I struggled so much in the workplace. How could a faith I felt so strongly be so overtaken at work? I confessed my potty mouth and the fact that with how I spoke, most who worked with me would probably be shocked to know I had written a book called *Grace and Peace*. I cried out to God asking, "What is wrong with me?"

It was then, as I lay with tears streaming down my face soaking my pillow, that I heard Him respond in a gentle whisper. "My daughter, I gave you My peace so you could share it with the world, having experienced it firsthand. But I have not given you a pass. *Do. The. Work.*"

I lay very still in my bed. When God speaks to you, you know it. I kept repeating what I had heard over and over. "But I have not given you a pass. *Do. The. Work.*" What work? I fell asleep promising to do the work I had been told to do, but what was the work?

When I woke up the next morning, I knew. In my first book, *Grace and Peace*, one thing I talk about is how we can't fully experience God's grace if we are harboring any unforgiveness—of others or ourselves—in our hearts. God was telling me that I was harboring unforgiveness deep in my heart, and it was time to get to work on dealing with it.

After I knew what needed to be done, I felt physically sick. I knew things were about to get real, and honestly, I didn't know if I could deal with it.

CHAPTER 3

Selfie Addiction

We think a lot about ourselves, and we tend to think even more about what others think about us. Some of us even imagine that we definitively know what others think about us. And if we focus too long on these thoughts, we can even convince ourselves that these thoughts are reality. But truth be told, people are rarely thinking about us as much as we imagine.

Add to these thoughts social media. Now we have a place where people can "like," "follow," or even "love" us. In this world of social media, have you noticed the constant bombardment of selfies? Selfies (taking a picture of yourself) are everywhere! There seems to be a constant need to show everyone what we are doing and experiencing at every moment. Some use this as a way of staying connected or to document events with pictures, which in and of itself isn't bad if it stops there. But unfortunately, for many, it serves as an attempt to meet other needs. For some, it is the need to be seen; for others, it is a need for approval. Many others use it as an attention-getter. Any of these, or any combination of these, are ways to allow another human being to validate your self-worth. But here is the deal: You are a child of God, and He is the **only** one who has the right to validate and define you.

When we were formed in our mother's wombs, God created us perfectly. There were no mistakes. Each of us was given talents to use throughout our lives, and each of us is unique in our makeup. But we all also have free will and the curse of original sin (see Genesis chapters 2 and 3). This curse gives us a sinful nature; and we must be aware that the enemy, Satan, loves it when we mess up, and he constantly is tempting us to do so. He loves to whisper in our ears (or, at times, scream in our heads) that we are not enough. Add to this scenario the fact that people are capable of doing hurtful, even hideous, things to one another when they act on that sinful nature. The results of these hurtful, even hideous, deeds are wounded people. And I believe these wounds are what drive this need for validation of self-worth.

But there is good news! God saw what a mess our world was, yet He loved us so much that He sent a Savior—His Son, Jesus Christ—to die for us and be the ultimate sacrifice for our sins. In the Bible, it says, "God has purchased our freedom with His blood and has forgiven all our sins" (Colossians 1:14). Also, later in Colossians, it says, "You have died with Christ, and He has set you free from the evil powers of this world. So why do you keep on following the rules of the world…" (Colossians 2:20).

So Jesus has given us a new option. Because of His death and resurrection, we can now be free from both our own sins and the evil others have inflicted upon us. We do not have to remain in bondage to our wounds of the past. And we certainly do not have to rely on others for validation of our self-worth for the present.

The world is a fickle place—what is "in" or "acceptable" today will most likely change tomorrow. Even the people we surround ourselves with will change. Children grow up. Loved ones move away. Friends come and go, and eventually, some in our lives will pass away. If you look over the people who have come and gone in your life over the years, you will probably be shocked by the number. Self-worth carries way too much weight in how we conduct our day-to-day lives to assign its validation to someone who may or may not be there for the long haul.

There is only One who meets the criteria—being there yesterday, today, and tomorrow—who should define your self-worth. This is your Creator, God. So what does God say about you?

He calls you beloved (Romans 9:25).

You are His treasured possession (Deuteronomy 7:6).

You are His child (John 1:12; Romans 8:17).

You are free (Galatians 5:11).

You have been redeemed (Ephesians 1:7).

You have been and will be restored (Colossians 1:13–14; 1 Peter 5:10).

You have been and can be forgiven (Hebrews 10:17; 1 John 1:9).

So let's break this down a little further. First, if we are God's beloved and treasured possessions, we are valuable. Boom! Nothing is assigned the titles of "beloved" and/or "treasured" if it holds no value. Second, if we are His child, would it make sense for Him to want us to remain in a state of wounded hurt? Absolutely not! In Matthew, it says, "If you, sinful people, know how to give good gifts to your children, how much more will your heavenly Father give good gifts to those who ask Him" (Matthew 7:11). God is the parent of all parents, the perfect example of love of all loves. He is incapable of lying. So we can rest assured that this "gap" we fall into—the space where we reside between God's perfect will for us and the consequences of our free will—is not meant to be a place we remain in a state of wounded hurt.

Okay, I imagine that about right now, you are saying, "Well, that's great, Deanna. But that gap is exactly the place I am in! So what do I do now?" Well, let's go back to our list and see what else God says about us.

You are free. In Galatians, it says, "So Christ has really set us free. Now make sure that you stay free, and don't get tied up again in slavery to the law" (Galatians 5:1). Does this mean we can do whatever we want? No, because that would lead us back to slavery by living the same sinful life Christ saved us from. But it also doesn't mean we are now a slave to the law. So what does this mean? I believe it means two things: (1) Immediately upon accepting Jesus as our personal Savior, we are set free. We just have to believe it. (2) This freedom requires action, with us making sure that we stay free. We have to make choices that both support our new freedom going forward and rid our hearts of the hurts and/or trauma of the past. This isn't easy. As a matter of fact, if we try to do it with only our own strength, it is impossible! But that's the beauty of the situation. We no longer have to, nor should we, do anything with only our own strength anymore. To do so is the exact recipe for failure. Instead, in everything we do, we take Christ along with us. The Bible says, "I can do all things through Christ who strengthens me" (Philippians 4:13 NKJV). We need to believe this, call on Him, follow His lead, and do the work.

* * * * *

Back in 2018

"Do. The. Work." This phrase heard while praying kept going over and over in my mind. As I got ready to meet with my friend Connie, who was helping me with my book's social media page, I decided I probably needed to seek prayer for understanding from some trusted Christians. So I shared with Connie, at a very high level without too much detail, that I was struggling. She told me that I should check out something called Fresh Start. When I asked her what Fresh Start was, she explained that it was a group that met every Tuesday to biblically work through their wounds and grievances.

Great, I thought. *Another "woe is me" self-help group. Just what I don't need—to sit around listening to people making excuses for their behaviors or, just as bad, feeling sorry for themselves. No, thanks.*

But instead, what I said as I smiled sweetly was "Thanks, I'll pray about that." I obviously was going to do no such thing. I groaned inwardly as I thought, "Really? Now I am lying about praying?"

The next day was Sunday, and I had decided I was going to find a couple of ladies at church whose power of prayer I knew to be spot on. After service, I got together with them, and they prayed over me. I just knew God was going to answer us! When the praying was over, one of the ladies, Sally, looked me square in the eye and said, "You need to go to Fresh Start. You need to process some of this that's in your heart." What? I could not have been more shocked if she would have poured a glass of water over my head. It was like she had been reading my mind as I thought over the previous day's experience. I knew in my heart that this was confirmation of what I should do, but in no way did I want to believe it. The last thing I wanted to do was go to this group.

"Well, that's kind of funny you would say that," I responded. "Yesterday, I was at a meeting with a friend that goes to a different church, and she said the same thing."

"That's not funny, my friend," Sally replied. "That's confirmation!"

"I'm actually good," I replied to Sally. "I don't even know what I would process if I went," I added nonchalantly.

"Pray about it," Sally advised with a gentle pat on my shoulder and a knowing nod of her head. "God will show you." And with that, she proceeded to give me the day, time, and location of the next meeting. I smiled and thanked her graciously. But on the inside, I was groaning again.

Really? I thought. *Ugh! I do not want to do this!* But right now, it didn't seem like God was interested in what I wanted to do. After all, wasn't doing what I wanted and handling everything as I saw fit what got me here to begin with? Obviously, **my** plan wasn't working. But this? Really? I resigned myself that I had to go, but I was definitely not on board with it.

That Tuesday night, however, I showed up at the church where Fresh Start was held. As I walked in the door, there was a table set up to sign in and get a name tag. As I went to write my name on the sticker, an extremely happy and bubbly woman welcomed me.

"Good evening! Is this your first time with us at Fresh Start?" The happiness was oozing from her and making me feel a little nauseated.

"Yes, it is," I replied with little to no enthusiasm. I did not feel that encouraging her was a wise thing to do.

"Well, welcome! It's never too late for a Fresh Start!" she beamed as though she just might burst with excitement. I, in turn, headed for the nearest restroom because I thought I just might vomit. *Good grief!* I thought. *Who talks like that?*

As I sat in the empty bathroom, I took some deep breaths. I thought, *What the heck did I just get myself into?* and prayed, "Please, God, help me do this!" I then washed my hands, took a deep breath, and walked out of the bathroom.

I took a wide detour, avoiding the lady at the sign-in table, and headed to the refreshments. Right or wrong, food has always been my friend, and I needed something to do. I did not want anyone noticing me standing alone and feeling they should talk to me because of it. I needed time to get a lay of the land and figure out what and who these people were.

The people serving refreshments seemed normal. Whew! Good call to get food. I headed to a table. The food actually looked good, and I hadn't had any dinner, so I was hungry. But more importantly, if I had food in my mouth, these people would probably leave me alone. After all, it's rude to ask people to speak with food in their mouths, right?

Wrong! I had no more than put a forkful of food into my mouth when another woman approached me. "Welcome to Fresh Start! Is this your first time here?" Although the saccharine wasn't dripping quite as thickly as it was from the woman at the sign-in table, it was still there in large quantity.

I gulped down my mouthful of food, being cognizant to not choke, and replied, "Yes, it is. Thanks." Maybe if I kept it brief, she would pick up that I really didn't want to engage at this time.

"Oh well, it's never too late for a Fresh Start!" As she put her things down and pulled out the chair next to me, she asked (without asking), "Do you mind if I sit with you?" I thought, *Do I have a choice?* In less than a moment, she had plopped down and started to chat.

Internally, I groaned yet again. Seriously? What had I gotten myself into? The woman continued to chat, and I realized I really didn't even know what she was saying. Just as I was getting concerned, as she asked me a question and then realized I hadn't listened to a word she had said, I spied Sally. *Oh, thank goodness!* I thought.

"Excuse me," I said as I jumped up. "I see my friend is here, and I just want to say a quick hello before we start." Without waiting for a reply, I went over to speak with Sally.

After a quick hello, Sally gave me a quick layout of what to expect. There would be two sessions: a large group where Doug, one of the leaders, would speak to all of us, and then a breakout session. In the breakout session, you either went to your assigned small group or remained in the larger group for a lesson. I wasn't assigned to a small group, so I would be staying with the large group. There would be a slight intermission between the two time slots to allow people to move to their groups, and refreshment refills and/or bathroom breaks.

"Okay," I told myself, "I can do this. If they are speaking, nobody is going to be coming directly at me." I started to calm down a bit. At about this time, Doug called the room to order and asked everyone to take their seats. Sally's table was already full, so I made my way back to my table and the woman who talked nonstop.

By this time, more people had seated themselves at my table and upon sitting down, I realized the table was completely full. All eyes were on Doug because he was starting the meeting.

As I listened to Doug speak, all I could think was, "Boy, this guy is fake." After all, **nobody** is that happy! With the tone of his voice, his ear-to-ear smile, and his chant of "Forgiven, forgiving, free," this guy made the saccharine lady seem mild. Everyone was saying, "Forgiven, forgiving, free" like it was their personal mantra. What the heck? So far, I was not seeing why Sally or Connie would think this was the place for me.

After the welcomes and announcements were taken care of, Doug started preaching about forgiveness. He specifically started talking about the condition of our hearts and what was being stored in them. As he talked about exposing denial in our hearts, I felt myself being drawn in. Maybe under all this saccharine, there was a message I needed to hear. Even though I had decided to skip out at intermission, I now decided to see it through to the end. But I definitely was going to go into the bathroom and then out to get more food during the intermission so I wouldn't be drawn into any more awkward conversations during the break!

When the second session started, at least half of the group had left for their small groups. A verse that was both read and discussed wouldn't leave my mind. "For the mouth speaks out of that which fills the heart. The good man brings out of his good treasure what is good; and the evil man brings out of his evil treasure what is evil" (Matthew 12:34b–35 NASB95). As he talked about how what came out of our mouths gave insight into what was harbored in our hearts, I visibly cringed. Everything he was saying was hitting way too close to home. Then he took out posters with pictures showing the results of hearts stuffed with poison and pain and how those things manifested in our lives via bitterness, resentment, insomnia, bad dreams, addictions, depression, explosions of anger/rage, illness, fear, criticalness, and lying. It was as if he had been spying on me and knew some of my deepest issues.

This was it. God wanted me to clean out the bottom of my barrel, and I now couldn't deny that I really didn't want to do it. He wanted me to completely get rid of my heart issues—the really deep ones that I had long ago nailed shut. The ones that, even though I hadn't realized it before now, were running the show. God wanted me to be completely free, but I had work to do. I did not want to be at Fresh Start, and goodness knows I did not want to be with these people. But as much as I didn't want any of this, there was one thing I did know—I was where I was supposed to be.

CHAPTER 4

Put in the Correct Lens

Isn't it funny that two people can experience the exact same thing and come away with two different versions of the situation? Or, if they do agree on a version of what happened, that it can affect each (if it even does) completely differently? How can this be? I believe this goes back to the free will God gives us. With each event that happens in our lives, we must decide how we are going to view it and how we are going to let it shape our present and/or future. I recognize from personal experience that this is easy to put on paper and not always so easy to do in reality. But nobody said this life was going to be easy. As a matter of fact, Jesus said, "I have told you all this so that you may have peace in Me. Here on earth you will have many trials and sorrows. But take heart, because I have overcome the world" (John 16:33).

Right now, some of you may be rolling your eyes at me. I can hear you saying, "Yeah, that's easy for you to say. You don't have any idea about the trauma I experienced at the hands of _____." And you would be right. Each of our stories is completely unique. But to be clear, I have experienced real trauma. I have been the victim of molestation, rape, infidelity, loved ones' suicide attempts, and doctor malpractice. I also have experienced serious medical issues and financial hardships. And that is the short list. So I truly do get the magnitude of my statement. The trauma inflicted on us by others, and sometimes by our own poor decisions, can leave very deep scars.

But this really leads to the point I am making. These trauma-induced wounds/scars can be horrific, and **none** of us would ever sign up for them to be inflicted upon us. So doesn't it make sense that we do everything we can to rid ourselves of their lasting power in our lives? Let me be clear: unresolved trauma—whether it was done by others or self-inflicted—is powerful. Sometimes that power is overt and in your face, such as a loss of a home or a pregnancy resulting from a rape. But many, many times that power is subtle. And to me, that's the worst—the silent but deadly kind. What do I mean by "silent but deadly"? Why do I call it that?

The silent but deadly traumas are the ones that people don't talk about. They include horrors such as rape, molestation, and abuse, to name only a few. These are things society not only doesn't encourage victims to talk about, but if they do, many times people then shame the victims. They label them and even "re-victimize" them. People are uncomfortable with the trauma of others, and unfortunately, many people's answer to their discomfort is to stop being around victims. So now the victims may find themselves no longer invited to events or included in activities. This equates to forced isolation. The reality is that when you've been a victim of an ugly, life-changing trauma, the last thing you want to do is sign up for more trauma. Therefore, many people do what feels like self-protection—they push the trauma down deep within themselves to never be talked about again. This stuffing is an attempt to get rid of the pain and regain control of their own life when it seems all control of their life has been taken away. The problem is that this self-protection is never really achieved because in this closed-off status, the victim loses the ability to completely feel and live. It is impossible to truly contain trauma. Stuffed trauma just seeps out into their lives through other means. Some of the ways trauma is manifested in our lives include a quick and raging temper, insomnia, unexplained illness, fear, addictions, lying, criticalness of others, resentment, and depression. All these seriously impact a person's quality of life.

The first step in dealing with unresolved trauma is adjusting and putting in your correct viewing lens of the situation. What do I mean by that? It is important to (1) recognize that unresolved trauma/issues are in your heart but (2) understand that you don't have to remain a victim. You can actively pursue healing. Adjusting your view might sound like an easy step, but my experience is that it can be the hardest because of underlying control issues that have come into play. Most people in this situation have worked **very** hard to regain control of their lives. Some are even quite proud of the survival skills they developed to be able to carry on. It's almost like those skills become a sort of "badge" that shows they are strong. Becoming a controller is something many people, including me, take on to be able to move forward. You don't really have to wonder if you have stepped into this role. Just ask your friends and family; they will tell you if they haven't already! But here's the secret most don't realize about control: There is no freedom in it. To give up control is the scariest step most victims will ever take, and because of this fear, it can be the hardest step of all.

* * * * *

Back in 2018

When I woke up, I remained in my bed and pondered what had transpired the previous evening at the Fresh Start meeting. Outside of Connie and Sally, I really wasn't a fan of the people there. But I had learned through the course of the meeting that there were other leaders, and Sally's husband, Douglas (not to be confused with Doug, the other leader), was one of them. I knew Douglas from church. Douglas was someone I not only liked but deeply respected. So maybe, just maybe, it was I who was being overly judgmental.

Okay, I thought, *God, you are going to have to help me here.* And with a commitment to return the next week, I put it out of my mind.

The following week when I returned, I was ready. I knew what to expect and no longer felt uncertain. I was in control!

I walked up to the sign-in table, grabbed a name tag, signed in, and ever so sweetly said "Hello, good to see you again" to the sign-in lady. I left the table before she could utter a word. *Yes!* I thought to myself, *I've got this*. I then noticed Connie at a table and marched over to it. "Can I sit with you guys?" I asked. "Sure," she replied. *Perfect,* I thought as I put my stuff down on the table. *No weird strangers.* I was feeling quite pleased with myself for how I was navigating this group. Connie then proceeded to tell me she couldn't really talk at that time because she was giving her testimony that night and was going over for prayer. I assured her I was fine and was just going to go get some food before everything started.

As I waited in the food line, I started to breathe a little easier. The people both serving the food and in line seemed normal, even pleasant. Maybe this wasn't going to be quite as bad as I had imagined. After getting my food, I returned to the table. Even though I didn't know anyone else outside of Connie and her husband, the others seemed very normal. After quick introductions around the table, people were engaged in their own conversations, and I was perfectly okay with that; it gave me time to assess the room and situation more.

Since it was the second week, I now knew what to expect—greeting, announcements, large group with testimonies and music, break, and then large group teaching or small group, depending on what you were assigned. I also now knew that if you wanted to be in a small group, you had to register and then wait to be chosen for one. The small groups were where all the personal counseling took place. I now knew this was what God wanted me to partake in, and because I didn't want to do this any longer than needed, I decided to jump off the high board and sign up. By the time I found the correct form, completed it, and turned it in, it was time for the session to start.

This time, when the large group teaching started, it wasn't Doug teaching. It was Pastor Steve. Although I had never heard him teach before, I did know of him because I had met his daughter several times. I had only heard good things. Plus, he was one of the founders of Fresh Start, so I was very interested to hear what he had to say.

One of the helpers was handing out some sheets of paper to use when following along with the teaching. When I looked at the title of what he would be speaking about, I gulped hard. Vows and Judgments. I thought, *Oh boy, looks like he might be going for the jugular straight out of the gate!*

Pastor Steve opened by saying, "A vow spoken out of a heart of love is not a burden, but a blessing. There is great power in a vow." But then he went on to say, "A vow spoken out of hurts, wounds, or bitterness is also a very powerful thing. You need to ask the Lord: Are there any vows in you of a destructive kind?"

Whoa! Although I hadn't really studied vows before, I knew enough to know that they were the "I will never" and "I will always" types of statements. I knew that many times they were statements of control and putting trust in self. I also knew that I had made several of these over the course of my life.

Pastor Steve went on to say, "When we make a vow in the face of being wounded, we have made an inner promise not to get close to others or to allow ourselves to be in a position to be abandoned." He also went on to say, "There are vows that many of us make that in some ways protect us, or so we think. The only thing more tragic than how we've been hurt is how we respond to it."

At this point, I checked out of listening for a moment. I was overwhelmed. It was like he knew what was going on in the secret parts of me. I glanced down at the handout to look like I was still following along, but a paragraph in the handout literally seemed to jump off the page at me. It read:

> God takes our hearts seriously. God's heart is broken as well. The choices we make, the person we become, the life we live or don't live, depend on how we handle it. When we try to protect or preserve our heart, we usually end up hurting ourselves more. To choose to shut our hearts to love is to deny the very thing that we were made for. We were made for relationship—to love and to be loved. To choose to shut down is to deny this very thing.

My mind flooded with vows I had made over the years that came rushing back. "I will never allow a man to hurt me again." "I won't date until my children are grown—I'm not good at it." "I will never allow doctors alone with my children." And the biggie, "No one will be allowed close enough to hurt me with their judgments again." I knew there were many more—too many to process.

I now knew why God wanted me here. In an attempt to protect both myself and my children, I had actually put us in a control prison. I was trying to control everything that could happen to us, to ensure that not only would I not be "re-victimized," but also that my children would be safe from experiencing trauma. Unfortunately, this was an unrealistic goal because nobody can control everything that happens to themselves and their loved ones. So when things ended up happening, I doubled down and closed the hatches harder in an even greater attempt to control life instead of dealing with the events rationally.

It was like the fog was being lifted from my eyes. I suddenly could see that what I had thought was safe was instead isolation and seclusion. What I had thought was protection was oftentimes overbearing and stifled growth. What I had thought was godly was actually controlling and, even worse, judgmental. My heart was breaking. With the realization of all of this, I found myself wondering, "How do you know when good is bad?"

CHAPTER 5

When Good Is Bad

One of my pastors, Pastor Mike McLaughlin, said once, "A good thing becomes a bad thing when it replaces the **main** thing." At that time, he was referencing social media. However, I believe it can be applied to most situations. Let me give you an example: You need to lose weight, so for health reasons you start to diet (good thing). You reach your goal, but in the process, you have developed an eating disorder (bad thing). So now your good thing (diet) has become a bad thing (eating disorder) because it replaced the main thing (healthy lifestyle). Does that make sense?

To understand where I'm going with this, let's talk a little more about trauma. There are three types of trauma:

1. Acute trauma: This results from a single stressful or dangerous event.
2. Chronic trauma: This results from repeated and prolonged exposure to highly stressful events. Examples include cases of child abuse, bullying, or domestic violence.

3. Complex trauma: This results from exposure to multiple traumatic events.

When any of these traumas occur, it is very important that, first and foremost, the victim secures safety. In the instance of chronic trauma, by definition, this has not happened immediately. It cannot be brushed aside that if this is not happening (securing safety), that in and of itself complicates things. The first step in dealing with trauma is understanding the type of trauma you are dealing with in your life and securing safety from it.

I am not a doctor nor do I profess to be. However, I **am** a survivor of all three types of trauma. And I am here to tell you there is freedom from the private, personal hell trauma can and many times does condemn you to. If you are reading this and you are presently experiencing trauma at the hands of another person, the absolute first thing you need to do is seek safety to stop the trauma. Call the police, go to a shelter, call a hotline. Do not stop until you are safe! I once called a priest but was told it was his bedtime and to call back in the morning. **This was not helpful or okay!** So when you are looking for help in securing safety, **do not stop until you are safe!** If the advice you receive is from a "respectable" person with a "respectable" title or position, but it is not leading you to safety—don't listen to this person and move on. Do whatever it takes to get yourself safe from additional trauma to be able to start the healing process. See the back of this book for a list of possible resources to turn to for help.

Let's talk for a moment about safety. Safety isn't just about being protected from others wishing to harm you.

Sometimes, safety means finding a place to live because the trauma made you homeless. Making sure you are safe means that your very basic needs are met: You are safe from physical/mental harm, and have shelter, food, clothing, and a way to support yourself financially, even if it is meager. In the beginning, sometimes this is accomplished through the generosity of others, but that is not a long-term solution. All of these necessities must be in place because if they are not, you are still in the throes of trauma and you have to get out of trauma before you can truly start the healing process of being set free from it.

It is normal for people to "batten down the hatches" once they are safe from trauma. What do I mean by that? You shut down. People may say to you, "You don't act the same. You never smile anymore. Where's the fun ______ (add your name in the blank)? You have changed." And guess what? They would be right. Trauma changes people! And no one hates it more than the people who had it happen to them. I personally call this the transition period. It's a time when lots of things are happening, many times all at once. You are realizing the trauma is over but may feel like you are in a fog of disbelief that it truly is over or even that it happened at all. Because your trust system has been severely broken, it may be hard to believe and accept that you really are truly safe.

What does this disbelief look like? If your trauma was person induced, it typically manifests in a severe lack of trust in people and many times results in closing off from people. But what about if your trauma wasn't person induced? What does it look like then? If your trauma was financially induced or severely affected your finances, you might find yourself excessively tight with your money—in extreme cases, even to the point of hoarding. Or you might find that you deny yourself simple pleasures that you can afford but refuse to allow because of "what could happen." (Side note: This is not advocating for spending outside of your means. Instead, this looks like the person who can afford to treat themselves—big or small—but doesn't because they are afraid it will mean they will have nothing to live on later. It is a form of extreme thinking.) During this transition period, trauma victims are using all of their resources to figure out how to live and successfully get on with life the best they can with what they have left.

Every survivor of trauma I have met does so by creating survivor skills. Utilizing them seems to be the next step. But this is where things can go very wrong. Typically, a survivor skill starts off as a good thing, because most times it is the victim's way to set boundaries to protect against re-victimization while healing. For someone who now has financial insecurity as a result of the trauma experienced, it may be a budget with very strong controls attached to it. For someone who was harmed physically and/or mentally by another, it may be strict scrutiny on who is allowed into the victim's personal life. These are just two examples—there are many more. But the point is that in the beginning, the victim needs these survival skills to be able to move on. When you have suffered severe trauma, moving on is very difficult. Trust, if there is any, is at an all-time low. With no trust for others, you are alone. And when you feel completely alone, the world can be a pretty cold and even terrifying place.

So cue in control. Control is most survivors' friend, at least that is what they think. It is easy for it to become the primary survival skill and, if not checked, the director of the survivor's life. Control takes the original survival skills and puts them on steroids. Take the budget example mentioned earlier. The strong budget (good) becomes so rigid it allows no deviation (bad). Now the goal of a healthy financial situation (main thing) has been hijacked by a budget (good thing) that has gone overboard and become a self-inflicted prison due to over-controlling behavior (bad thing).

Let's try another example. A person has been sexually abused. Going forward, the goal would be to never be abused again (main thing). The survivor skill employed is to set up strong boundaries for relationships in the victim's life (good thing). Control steps in and replaces boundaries with walls to keep most people out (bad thing). Now the survivor is living life mostly alone within a new type of prison. A good thing becomes a bad thing when it replaces the main thing. The Bible says, "It is for freedom that Christ has set us free. Stand firm, then, and do not let yourselves be burdened again by a yoke of slavery" (Galatians 5:1). When control takes dominance in a person's life, balance leaves and imprisonment follows. Unfortunately, many don't even realize the prison they are in.

* * * * *

Back in 2018

I woke up drenched in sweat. My heart was racing. Another nightmare. This was becoming a daily event. I knew better than to try to go back to sleep. To do so would allow the dream to continue, as they had done many times in the past. This particular dream was about the man (in his twenties) who had raped me when I was seventeen. Out of all my recurring dreams from past traumas (there were about five variations), I hated this particular one the most. Every time, I woke up feeling as if it had just happened again. Every time, I woke up feeling that it was my fault. Every time, I had to calm myself and remind myself that I was safe and a good person. This time was no different.

Ugh! When will this stop? I now knew that these issues of my past were exactly what God wanted to deal with. Well, I'd had it. *You want it, God? Well, take it, then,* I thought angrily to myself, *because I'm **over** it!*

The day before, I had received the call. I had been selected for a small group at Fresh Start and needed to decide who/what I was going to process. You would think it would have been the rape/rapist. But deep in my heart, I knew I couldn't go straight there. It was too big. That would require a mountain of trust for this group that they needed to earn. And heaven knows I had experienced enough traumatic things in my life that I had plenty of options to choose from for Fresh Start. So I decided to make a list and pray over it. I would let God show me what/whom to process. After all, this was His idea anyway.

I ended up going with a much lesser yet recurring issue with one of my sisters that God showed me needed resolving. Being from a family of eleven kids, it is common to not be close to all of your siblings. But the issues in this relationship went way beyond not being close. We could barely be in the same room together before issues arose. And it had become generational now—our children also struggled in a way they didn't struggle with their other cousins. I knew this was not what God desired of me, but I had never been able to get over the feelings of hurt, betrayal, rejection, and judgment that had accumulated over the years. The more I prayed, the more I knew this was what needed to be processed first. Anyone who knew both of us very well knew there was an ongoing issue and most probably even had an opinion as to who was more at fault. The wounds were deep and the transgressions great…so much so that it was one of the five issues that gave me recurring nightmares. God wanted this heart issue resolved, and on this freedom journey, it seemed as good of a place to start as any.

The following Tuesday, I returned to Fresh Start. Over the weeks since I had started attending, I had settled down. I knew the routine of the agenda, and even though the teachings were solid, I still kept primarily to myself. Except for the couple of people I had already known, I hadn't opened up to connect with anyone else. The people still seemed a little fake to me. After all, who really is that stinking happy? By now, I knew the teaching was good, but I just wished they would tone down the syrupy talk.

But tonight would be different. Tonight, I would start in a small group. So instead of staying in the large group for the second half of the session, I, along with three other ladies, would be joining three counselors in a small group. We would be meeting every week for approximately three months.

As we started, the first thing we did was to review the Fresh Start Processing Group Statement of Understanding. It had three parts to it: Commitment, Process, and

Guidelines. The Commitment and Process parts were just as you would expect—giving the details of meeting time, whom to call if you had to miss, how many weeks it would last, etc. But the Guidelines portion was very interesting. It stressed that coaching and encouragement would be provided by Fresh Start Group Leaders only, with Group Participants not giving advice or input to other Participants. It also stressed that the Fresh Start Group is a safe, caring environment, and confidentiality must be maintained, just as anyone would expect in a group such as this. But the interesting part was that it also stressed that Fresh Start Groups are not counseling sessions but instead are groups designed to help each individual process his/her offense, hurt, loss, and/or traumatic event, and then ultimately experience forgiveness and/or freedom from the debilitating effects of the trauma or loss. This stopped me in my tracks. You see, I had tried counseling sessions before, and although they had helped me through the moment, they had never once given me freedom. With trying so hard to control my life, I didn't even think freedom was an option for someone like me. Survival was all I could imagine. Moving on and forward was always the goal. Freedom never entered the equation.

Do. The. Work. I now finally understood that "the work" was my journey to complete healing. And complete healing was my path to freedom.

CHAPTER 6

You Are Always on Your Mind

You cannot believe how many times in my past I have been certain I knew exactly what someone was thinking about me. Many of you have shared with me the same sentiment. Isn't it interesting that when we think these things, it is rare when we believe someone is thinking good thoughts about us?

Typically, the scenario goes something like this: _______ doesn't like me. He/she never talks to me or invites me to do anything. There are millions of variations of this scenario, but essentially, the thought process goes like this: There is someone you care about or wish to know better. For some unknown reason, the relationship has stalled somewhat (or a lot) or not proceeded at all. Instead of proactively seeking the person out to see if there is an actual problem, your mind goes into overdrive and fills in the blanks with negative thoughts. If you don't take your thoughts captive, you can convince yourself the thoughts are the real confirmed story and not just assumptions you have created in your own head.

It is common for trauma victims to overplay or over-think things. Another scenario could be looking back on something you've done that you wished you hadn't and believing that **everyone else** is thinking about it and talking about it all the time.

Spoiler alert: You are never on the minds of others even a fraction of the time you are on your **own** mind.

Say it loud for those in the back. Say it louder for those imprisoned by trauma. The harm we do to ourselves by letting our minds and "self-talk" run rampant is unbelievable. Jesus said, "For whatever is in your heart determines what you say. A good person produces good words from a good heart, and an evil person produces evil words from an evil heart. And I tell you this, that you must give an account on judgment day of every idle word you speak. The words you say now reflect your fate then; either you will be justified by them, or you will be condemned" (Matthew 12:34b–37).

Words have power. And it's not just what we say to others or about others. What we say to and about ourselves is powerful, too, maybe the most powerful. Let's look at another example. Let's look at the story in Mark 5 regarding the woman with the issue of blood. The Bible says this woman had been hemorrhaging for **twelve years**! Can you imagine?!? Most of us think a week is bad. Yikes! I'm sure you, as well as I, can relate—this woman was desperate to be healed. And she knew this man, Jesus, could be the answer. But seriously—this had been going on for twelve years. She **had** to also have been battling doubts. And it probably would have been much easier to assume this was her fate in life. To completely understand what that fate meant in those days, you need to know that a woman was considered unclean while bleeding. The status of being labeled "unclean" would have excluded her from most social contact because if others touched her, or anything she sat or laid on, they would be labeled "unclean" too. This was about much more than the inconvenience of bleeding for twelve years. This was about living what probably seemed like a life sentence—a life in solitary confinement, always watching but never being allowed to participate. Yet sometimes the lack of hope in our lives can make us desperate to do something, anything, to make a change. We may even become a little reckless to make a change. After twelve years, hope had to have gone out the window long ago. Hope dashed is painful; the disappointment can be crushing. Let's see what the woman in the Bible did:

> And there was a woman in the crowd who had had a hemorrhage for twelve years. She had suffered a great deal from many doctors through the years and had spent everything she had to pay them, but she had gotten no better. In fact, she was worse. She had heard about Jesus, so she came up behind him through the crowd and touched the fringe of His robe. For she thought to herself, 'If I can just touch His clothing, I will be healed.' Immediately the bleeding stopped, and she could feel that she had been healed! (Mark 5:24–29)

What? Can you imagine? What no doctor had been able to accomplish in twelve years (and, might I add, while taking all of her money in their attempts), Jesus did with a touch to the fringe of His robe! But let's look closer at the passage—a couple of things had to happen first: (1) She had to take captive her thoughts. She couldn't live in the negative land where all past attempts had failed. She had to believe this attempt was worth trying because it would work. Note: "I will be healed" was what she said to herself, not "I might be healed" or "maybe I will be healed." She chose to stand strong in her self-talk before it happened to give no room for the enemy to engage her in doubt. (2) She took action. She couldn't let her past experiences and outcomes dictate her current ones. To sit idle and wish for something to change never brings change. Even when our current circumstances are a direct result of what someone else has done to us, we still cannot allow ourselves to become defeated and content with inaction. "If I can just touch His clothing, I will be healed." She figured out what she needed to do and did it! Let's go back to the Bible and see what happened next:

> Jesus realized at once that healing power had gone out from Him, so He turned around in the crowd and asked, "Who touched My clothes?" His disciples said to Him, "All this crowd is pressing around you. How can You ask, 'Who touched Me?'" But He kept on looking around to see who had done it. Then the frightened woman, trembling at the realization of what had happened to her, came and fell at His feet and told Him what she had done.

> And He said to her, "Daughter, your faith
> has made you well. Go in peace. You have
> been healed." (Mark 5:30–34)

Jesus knew who had touched Him; He didn't call her out for His knowledge. He called her out for **her**. Look closer—she is described as "the frightened woman." This is another side effect of trauma—many times the victim of trauma is left in a frightened state, where a life of hiding things (shame, isolation, hurt, truth) becomes the norm. But Jesus didn't leave her there in her fear. Because He called her out, she had a choice. She could run away and remain in her fear, or she could muster all her courage and step forward to tell Him what she had done. It had to be hard; she didn't know what He would do. Would He reject her? Would He be angry? And worse, would this miracle worker take back His miracle of healing? That fear in and of itself would have made many run away. She didn't know the answer, but "trembling," she still stepped forward and "told Him what she had done." What did He do?

He took away her fear and replaced it with peace. He said, "Daughter, your faith has made you well. Go in peace. You have been healed." God does not want us living in fear or in a controlled prison. She needed to know this, and she could only truly know by speaking her truth and owning it. This would allow Him to release her from the questioning in her mind and give her the peace she so desperately needed. This would allow Him to validate her faith and reaffirm her healing. She could now personally and publicly fully realize she was healed. Her mind could finally rest in His peace.

* * * * *

Back in 2018

It was time. The first half of the Fresh Start session was over, and it was time to go into small groups. Suddenly, I felt as if I might throw up. I thought, "What am I doing? I don't know these people. How can I be sure they aren't going to get diarrhea of the mouth and start sharing my private information all over the place? Gosh, nowadays there is even the internet—what if it shows up there?" My mind was racing, and I couldn't make it stop. The desire to duck out a side door and leave was overwhelming.

Get yourself together! I thought as I forced myself to walk through the classroom door where we would be meeting. Throughout my life, I had developed an "armor" I put on whenever I felt threatened by somebody and/or a situation. That "armor" consisted of a strong, almost domineering front. It sometimes included being loud; it usually included volunteering to do whatever no one else was willing to do (because of fear or common sense), and it always put me in control (even to the peril of myself). I felt the "armor" come on as the group leaders were asking for volunteers to go first in sharing. *Get it over with,* I thought.

"I'll go first," I said as I noticed another woman had also raised her hand to volunteer.

"Thanks, Deanna. We are going to let Faith go first because she has been through this before. We will let you go second. That way you can see how the format of the process works."

"Okay!" I said brightly. But I didn't feel lighthearted. Actually, I wasn't quite sure how I felt. The need to control the situation, even down to the order of when I took my turn, was high. But at the same time, I felt a new feeling—**relief**! Someone else was very much in control here and making sure I wasn't going to sabotage this. The problem was that these two feelings—lack of control and relief at not being in control—were at war within me.

Good grief! I thought to myself. *Do these ladies even have a clue as to what they are getting themselves into? I am one messed-up puppy!*

As I listened to Faith tell her story, my heart thawed. Initially, when I found out three others were going to hear my story, I was extremely uncomfortable. After all, I certainly didn't need their judgment or pity. But as I listened to Faith, my heart broke for her and what she had been through. The first part of the process is describing who or what has offended or hurt you, or who or what you have lost. Then you describe how you have been affected, and finally, how you have responded to this specific offense, hurt, or loss. As you can imagine, it doesn't get any more soul-bearing and personal than this. All of this must be prepared in writing, in advance, so it can be read. As Faith read hers, I saw right away that this was a good strategy; it made one more reflective and helped to not lose key facts due to high emotions caused by recounting the events. The other thing I noticed was that these group leaders really cared about Faith. There was no judgment; as a matter of fact, they empathized with her and validated her feelings.

They told her they were so sorry she'd had to go through what she had been through, and it was genuine.

At the end of the session, they reminded me I would be next the following week. Once everyone had gone through these first three steps, it would go back to Faith, and we would repeat the order for the last three steps. I felt relief wash over me. Boy, was I glad I was second and not first!

The next day, I sat down to do my homework for the next week. I knew I had to tackle this assignment quickly and not procrastinate. Every day I put off doing the assignment would tempt me further to back out of the whole thing altogether.

In the small group, I had been given a booklet with questions to help walk participants through preparing to tell their story. I decided to tackle this like a homework assignment. With a methodical mindset, I went about answering the questions. What I didn't prepare for was the bombardment of emotions that hit. All of a sudden, I was transported back to being that little girl who idolized her beautiful sister and just wanted her to be her best friend.

Then *bam*! I was the prepubescent child feeling vulnerable and confused by her sister's actions. And before I could catch my breath, I was the angry teenage girl who pretended not to give a crap but inside was dying from the betrayal and double standards she was living when it came to me daily. From a young adult who didn't care anymore to an older adult who couldn't care anymore—all the emotions hit me hard, like a movie I didn't want to watch. This was a box that hadn't been opened, much less explored, in a very long time, and the range of emotions that overtook me threatened to topple me.

As I finished my assignment, tears streamed down my face. I now understood the nightmares I had concerning my sister. I knew this was not what God wanted me to store deep in my heart. I knew He wanted it cleaned out—gone once and for all. But I had no idea how to get from here to there. And if I couldn't do it on this topic, how in the heck would I ever be able to do it concerning the rape? My heart was heavy. I didn't have the answers. But I knew who did.

CHAPTER 7

Lose the Scales

The one consistent thing about trauma is you learn instantly not to trust, and this includes anyone and everyone. Misplaced trust is what got you here in this place to begin with, right? I mean, you should be able to trust your parents to keep you safe, right? That is, after all, their primary job. If something happens to you on their watch, they failed. Or maybe it's your siblings. You should be able to trust that they will have your back, defend you against others, and be willing to coach you and have any needed hard conversations while remaining in your corner, right? So if they aren't there for you or join in with others against you, or even worse, are the instigator of believing the worst about you and spreading it; well, they failed the trust test too. What about your doctor? You should be able to go to your doctor (or take your children to a doctor) and not worry that anyone is going to be abused. But if something inappropriate happens, they, too, have failed the trust test. How about your boss? I mean your boss most definitely holds a position of power over you. If he/she mistreats you or allows others to mistreat you, isn't that a violation of trust? What about your children? After pouring into them and loving them for years, isn't it a breaker of trust if they no longer have time for you in their life? How about pastors or priests? If you go to them for help, and they shine you on or are inappropriate, isn't that a direct violation of trust? And then there's your spouse. If they are not faithful or truthful or are unwilling to fight for you and your relationship, isn't that an absolute break of trust? What about when a loved one tries to commit suicide? They actually tried to completely separate themselves from you forever. Isn't that a huge trust breaker? What about the stranger or acquaintance who sexually/physically/emotionally harms you? Does this give you the right to not trust? What about God, who allows some or all of these things to happen to you? Didn't He fail you? **Didn't He become the ultimate trust breaker?**

Yep, I just went there. Nope, it's probably not socially acceptable to do so. But it needed to be brought up. Why? Because many victims of trauma feel some or all of these statements to be true. And until we can get real—not only about what happened but how what happened left us feeling—we are never going to get to a place of healing. The world of healing has nothing to do with socially and/or politically acceptable speech. And guess what? God isn't interested in it either. Healing starts with raw and brutal honesty, with nothing covered up or sweetened. It can— no, it will—be tough, but I assure you God can handle it, and so can you. How do I know? Because I did, and I personally went through each and every one of these things. Not only can God handle this gut-level raw honesty, but

He already knows it all anyway. He knows everything about us, every dark secret or thought, so we might as well start being real with Him. The Bible says, "And you will know the truth, and the truth will set you free" (John 8:32).

Let's dig deeper into this. Are all those expectations reasonable expectations? Yes, it is reasonable to expect that you should be safe under the care of or in the company of your parents, siblings, doctors, bosses, spiritual leaders, spouse, loved ones, and friends. But reasonable by definition means as much as is appropriate or fair; moderate; fairly good; average. Additionally, it is defined (of a person) as having sound judgment; fair and sensible; based on good sense. Herein lies the problem. By definition, this means that the chance of this actually happening is only fairly good or average, not 100 percent certain. Isn't it also fair to say that for these situations, to have a reasonable expectation of outcome, we probably need to be dealing with reasonable people who have sound judgment, based on good sense? But that is not how all people are. Some people are evil, as that is the path they have chosen. And even people who have good intentions are fallible because we all sin. Every person has a story, and I believe if one took the time to trace it back, much could be understood. But wait, what about God? He certainly could have stopped all of this if He had wanted to. And yet He didn't. So why, if these are reasonable expectations and you have experienced trauma, would you trust Him again?

This is where we need to understand free will and remember the gap theory, which I learned from Fresh Start (freshstartforallnations.org).

God's Design

GAP

Your Experience

Because God gives all humans free will to make choices, not all choices made reflect God's desire for us. God's perfect design for our life would be for us to have loving parents and children, selfless friends, encouraging and uplifting teachers and spiritual leaders, caring bosses, ethical medical providers, etc. But your experience may be far from that picture, especially if you experienced trauma. The middle—between what God's perfect design for your life was and what you actually experienced—is the GAP. The GAP is everything that falls short of His perfect design and will for you. It's what you didn't get. The GAP is a result of sin. Sin causes others (and us) to fall short. Someone's sin (or our own) creates a gap in our life that causes our experience to fall short of His perfect design. Be certain of this: God is not okay with our trauma. Psalm 56:8 says, "You keep track of all my sorrows. You have collected all my tears in Your bottle. You have recorded each one in Your book." God is a tender-hearted Father! Psalm 56:9 goes on to say, "My enemies will retreat when I call to You for help. This I know: God is on my side!" What an encouraging passage. Not only is God not happy about our situation, but He is just waiting for us to use our free will to call on Him for help! He is on our side!

In John 11, we find one of Jesus' close followers and friends, Mary, in great sorrow and distress over the death of her brother Lazarus, whom Jesus also loved greatly. "When Jesus saw her weeping and saw the other people wailing with her, a deep anger welled up within Him, and He was deeply troubled. 'Where have you put him?' He asked them. They told Him, 'Lord, come and see.' Then Jesus wept" (John 11:33–35). Jesus experienced both anger and sorrow over the death of his friend Lazarus. But He didn't leave him in the grave. "Then Jesus shouted, 'Lazarus, come out!' And the dead man came out, his hands and feet bound in graveclothes, his face wrapped in a headcloth. Jesus told them, 'Unwrap him and let him go'" (John 11:43–44).

God does not want to leave us in the grave either! Just like Lazarus, our traumas and losses in life have our hands and feet bound in the graveclothes of fear and mistrust. Like Lazarus, our faces are wrapped in the headcloth of control. And like Lazarus, Jesus wants us to unwrap from these things and be let go. Jesus wants us to be free!

At this point, you may be saying, "Great, Deanna, but how do I do that?" By losing the scales. You know, those things we use to measure and keep track of all that has been done to us and by whom. We must be willing to step out in faith and trust God while we process our losses, sorrows, and traumas. We have to be willing to seek help from a biblical source and be vulnerable enough to walk through the steps of healing. We need to care more about getting healthy and restored with God than getting even with those who have wronged us. We must be willing to let go so that we can finally move forward.

* * * * *

Back in 2018

It was time. Tonight was my turn to share at Fresh Start. I felt nauseated. We had just been dismissed from the large group to go to our small groups, and part of me still wanted to duck out the side door.

"O Lord, please help me!" I threw the prayer up with feelings of desperation. The feelings of vulnerability threatened to overwhelm me.

As I walked in the door, Candace (one of the leaders) gave me a hug. She had prayed with me earlier, and the hug calmed me down. Once the group had prayed, we jumped right in, and it was my turn to speak. In the first step, you are asked to begin by identifying the area of offense, hurt, or loss in your life that you are going to process. You have to specifically list offenses or hurts and the person(s) involved. Then you have to list the loss that you had experienced in your life due to it. This part was easy—I had never had a problem talking about my issue with my sister. After all, in my opinion, she had wronged me in many ways, and many people over the years had agreed with me, reinforcing those thoughts and feelings. As I recounted the story, my voice was confident and steady.

As I came to the second step where I was to describe how I had been affected by the offense, loss, or hurt, my confidence eroded. I was supposed to describe what my thoughts had been—both about myself and toward the person(s) involved. Even more specifically, I was to describe how I had felt about the situation as a whole. This was where I would have to go deep into what I had been feeling.

I grabbed my water and took a big gulp, using the time to try to blink back tears. Just like when I was writing this information down, all the events of my past were playing in my mind like a movie. I hadn't wanted to live through it when I had lived it, I hadn't wanted to "watch" the replay as I prepared for this moment, and I certainly didn't want to "rewatch it" as I recounted my story to these people.

I paused from reading my story and looked up at the leaders with tears rolling down my cheeks. "I'm sorry" was all I could say.

One of the leaders said "It's okay" as she pushed a box of tissues toward me. Another leader said a quick prayer for me and asked if I was ready to resume. The love displayed in those simple actions gave me the strength to continue to describe how I was affected.

"How has this affected me? Well, I do not have high esteem for myself. I am the queen of 'fake it till you make it!' I struggle to think I am good enough or worthy of love from a good man. I constantly think that when people really get to know me, they won't like me, so I tend to isolate myself. As a teenager, I became very promiscuous and rebellious. I truly can go to the extreme if I am feeling judged." I paused. I now had to read my thoughts specifically about my sister. Tears streamed down my face as I read out loud. The reading of my feelings out loud took me down a road that transformed me. I was no longer the confident, accusing adult who had begun sharing earlier. The more I read, the more I traveled backward in time until I was just the little girl who wanted to be loved by her big sister.

The pile of used tissues continued to grow. I paused to take another drink and breathe a moment before starting the last section. As I did, the leaders encouraged me with comments of both empathy and encouragement. In the last step, I was to describe my response to the offense, hurt, or loss. I was to specifically own what I had said, what I had done, and what I had decided in my responses to the offense, hurt, or loss. The Bible verse used to help in preparing for this section is: "See if there is any offensive way in me and lead me in the way everlasting" (Psalm 139:24 NIV).

I gulped down the last of my water, wishing I had grabbed two glasses instead of one. I took a deep breath and continued reading. Sharing (and owning) that I am critical of my sister was hard. Owning out loud in front of others that at times I gossiped and judged her to others was embarrassing. Acknowledging that I had done this at times in front of my kids made me feel ashamed. Tears continued to stream down my face. I was not the only victim here.

"I thought that since my sister and I get along now as adults that everything was fine. But I keep having nightmares about her and in the nightmares, we are young again. I want the dreams to stop. I love my sister, and I want this in my past." As I closed my book with my notes in it, I felt a huge sigh of relief leave my body. I was done. I was an emotional wreck, but I had made it through.

I tentatively looked around the table at the rest of the group for the first time, expecting judgment or at least disdain. Instead, my gaze was met with compassion and love. The leaders praised me for my honesty and ended the meeting in prayer. Afterward, a couple of people asked if they could give me a hug. Begrudgingly, I allowed it. Although I greatly appreciated their compassion, I was raw and spent, and I really didn't have the bandwidth for all this touchy-feely stuff—even if the intentions were good.

"I'm really spent and exhausted," I apologized. "I just need to go home and go to bed. Thanks, everyone." I quickly grabbed my things and headed out the door. My mind was flying in a million directions, and I just wanted to be alone to sort through it all.

As I got into my car, my first thought was, *Man, I am glad I don't have to speak again for four weeks!* But that thought was immediately replaced with the decision that I needed to do my "homework"—the last three sections of the booklet—that weekend. Now that I was in the middle of this, I needed to finish. And that meant getting my part done and down in writing as soon as possible.

When the weekend arrived, I sat down to do my assignment. After a quick prayer, I opened the book to begin to write. There were three sections to prepare for the first night of sharing, and now I had three more sections to prepare for the final night. My hands were sweaty. I knew, as tough as the first part had been, this would be even tougher. I opened the book to continue on in part 4.

Part 4 in the process has you pouring out your heart to the Lord. You are required to write down exactly how you feel about everything that happened, including expressing any unmet desires, to the Lord—specifically calling out what you are disappointed or upset about, or wish would/ would not have happened. As I wrote down my thoughts, the wounded little girl who was so prevalent while preparing for my first night of sharing was replaced by the angry teenager. The more I wrote, the more the anger ripped through me. I was hot on fire as I turned the page and received the instructions to now express my current desires to the Lord and then to **give thanks to the Lord**! What? I threw my pen down. These people must be crazy! They expected me to actually **give thanks** for this crap? This heartache? This wound? I decided I had better pause and pray again because anyone who actually knew me would know that I was not about to give thanks for going through what I went through with my sister.

After praying, I took a deep breath and picked my pen back up. As it touched the paper, the words started flowing, and the tears started streaming down my face.

"I desire to be free from the bitterness, to be free from judgment, and to see my sister as Jesus sees her. I want to truly forgive her so my heart can be released from the pain. I want to be able to trust again. I no longer want to be the one who sees the train coming because I assume the worst is going to happen to me because it always has. I don't want people to compare me to Job; I want people to compare me to Paul! A changed woman! I want my heart to be healed, so I can trust both men and women again. And maybe, one day, become one with a godly man of God's choosing."

As I paused my writing, I realized that not only was the anger gone, but I was exhausted. It was time to give thanks, and I realized I no longer wanted to fight. As I reflected on some of the Scriptures written in the book, two of them seemed to leap off the page at me:

Offer to God a sacrifice of thanksgiving,
and pay your vows to the Most High; call

upon Me in the day of trouble; I shall rescue you, and you will honor Me... He who offers a sacrifice of thanksgiving honors Me; And to him who orders his way aright I shall show the salvation of God. (Psalm 50:14–15, 23 NASB1995)

And we know that God causes all things to work together for good to those who love God, to those who are called according to His purpose. For those whom He foreknew, He also predestined to become conformed to the image of His Son. (Romans 8:28–29 NASB1995)

It hit me like a ton of bricks. I wasn't being asked to give thanks for my circumstances as a happy thing. My thanksgiving was going to be a sacrifice to God—just as Jesus did at the cross. And in doing so, God was promising that when I call on Him in my trouble, He would rescue me. Not only that, but He would cause all of this hurt to work for good. In offering my suffering up as a sacrifice of thanksgiving, He would restore me. A light of hope turned on that I hadn't experienced in a very long time. I began to write:

Lord, I choose to give thanks for You knowing my heart and my struggle with this, and for some reason—whether by sin or design—You allowed it. So I give thanks as a sacrifice to You, as You, too, were betrayed, hurt, made fun of, and abandoned. You experienced every emotion I felt—both at the cross and while I was experiencing it—so although it hurt then and hurts now, I will thank you for allowing me the privilege of suffering beside You because You never left me. As a thanksgiving to You, I will remember that You work **all** things for good to those who love God, which means You will bring good out of this too. And I will accept out of thanksgiving whatever Your will is for this in my life. In Jesus' name, Amen.

I took a deep breath. The simple act of writing these words down already made me feel stronger and lighter all at the same time. I knew I had to forge on. The next section was titled "Forgive." It started with telling the "Parable of the Unforgiving Servant" in Matthew 18:21–35. If you haven't read it, stop now and do so. The gist of the story is that we can't ask God to forgive our sins and then think He is going to be okay with us not forgiving others. In the "Forgive" section, you are asked to write out your confession of unforgiveness to the Lord, along with the related wrong attitudes and/or responses.

As I wrote out my confession of unforgiveness, any remnants of self-righteousness dissolved. It was as though the Lord removed the shades from my eyes and took the scales I had been using all those years to judge my sister on and asked me to view myself with them. I didn't like what I saw.

The next step after writing out your confession of unforgiveness was to choose to forgive the person who has hurt or offended you. What previously seemed impossible, now seemed doable. Slowly I wrote down every offense— no matter how big or small—that I could remember holding against her. As I decided to forgive each one, I wrote a prayer to the Lord, expressing it not as a desire, as I had done at times in the past, but as a decision. As I finished, although I felt better, I was exhausted. But I also knew I still needed to continue.

The last section in the book is titled "Release." In this section, you are to entrust the person and/or the situation to the Lord in the form of a prayer. Two of the verses used for reflection spoke strongly to me:

> Live in harmony with one another. Do not be proud, but be willing to associate with people of low position. Do not be conceited. Do not repay anyone evil for evil. Be careful to do what is right in the eyes of everybody. If it is possible, as far as it depends on you, live at peace with everyone. Do not take revenge, my friend, but leave room for God's wrath, for it is written: "It is mine to avenge; I will repay," says the Lord. On the contrary: "If your enemy is hungry, feed him; if he is thirsty, give him something to drink. In doing this, you will heap burning coals on his head." Do not be overcome by evil,

but overcome evil with good. (Romans 12:16–21 NIV)

May the words of my mouth and the meditation of my heart be pleasing in your sight, O Lord, my Rock and my Redeemer. (Psalm 19:14 NIV)

After entrusting who or what you are entrusting to the Lord, you are asked to bless and pray for the person who has offended or hurt you. I took a deep breath. No longer was I feeling like an angry teenager or a hurt little girl. Instead, I was a tired, humbled adult who very much realized there were two victims here. And even more importantly, I realized none of what happened was God's plan for my life and that every time I had cried, He had shed tears too. He had hurt right along with me. I picked up my pen.

Lord, as of this moment I am renouncing the lies of the enemy. I will no longer believe that I am not worthy of love or to be fought for because You showed me I am by choosing me, by dying on the cross for me, even before I chose You. In my flesh, no, I am not worthy. But by Your cross, I am because I am a princess of the King…and my sister is too.

Father God, I am entrusting both my sister and myself and these situations to You. Heal both of us from these past experiences. Instead of my mind and heart remembering the offenses, fill me with the knowledge that she, too, was a wounded little girl who had also been harmed by others. Help me remember that although her journey was different from mine, it had pain too. She, too, suffered loss. Help me, Lord, as I start fresh from this moment, to not let jealousy seep into my heart. Help me not to compare our lives but to instead pray blessings on her. Show her what You desire of her as Your daughter and protect her from the lies of the enemy. Lord, I pray You would bless her with a job that brings her happiness and with strong Christian friends that would encourage her growth in You. Bless our relationship as sisters and may we grow closer in love as we age. Help our sisterly love to be defined not by life's circumstances and sin but by our mutual love for You. Bless us, heal us, hold us, and keep us in You. In Jesus' name, Amen.

I laid down my pen. It was done. I was finished. I was exhausted. But for the first time in my life, I felt empty—empty of anger and resentment, empty of the fight. Now all I had to do was wait for my turn to present this last half.

The next four weeks flew by. As I listened to the others in my group share their stories, the compassion in my heart grew. Although their stories were different, one thing was the same. All of us had been living a façade—trying to act like we were fine when we were far from it. We were living a lie and the people we all were lying the most to were ourselves.

Before I knew it, the night of my final processing where we go through the last three sections of the book was here. I had not looked at what I had written since I closed the book the night I wrote it. My nerves were on edge but not quite as bad as the first time I spoke—these ladies were no longer strangers.

As large group finished and we broke to go into small groups, a realization hit me. I no longer felt the need to duck out a side door. I smiled. A lot had changed over the last few weeks. Our group leader, Candace, gave me a side hug. She had prayed with me earlier and had become a trusted confidante.

Remembering the last time I had spoken, I quickly went over to the refreshment table and grabbed two glasses of water. As I filled the water, I realized how important the outcome of this evening was for me. Over the last few weeks I had 'hoped', and that I hadn't experienced in years—maybe ever.

"O Lord, please let this be real. Please complete the healing you started four weeks ago," I prayed silently as I made my way back to our meeting room.

Once in the room, things began quickly. After an opening prayer, I was asked to jump immediately into what I had written. Just like the first time I presented, the tears flowed. Just like the first time I presented, I received great empathy and compassion from the leaders. The fourth section of pouring out my heart went well. But as I finished the fifth section on forgiving, Candace called me out.

"Deanna," Candace said.

I stopped reading and looked up.

"That was very good, but you need to forgive your sister for everything. You need to choose to forgive her for rejecting you. You need to choose to forgive her for slandering you to people important to you."

I paused. I had listed so many things but realized I had omitted those—maybe the most important ones.

Candace went on. "It is important to get everything covered to allow no cracks for the enemy." I paused to gather my thoughts and turned them to the Lord. This had to be heartfelt and not a robot response to an instruction. As I prayed out loud to the Lord, it very much became my decision to choose to forgive my sister for rejecting me and to choose to forgive her for slandering me to people that were important to me.

It was time to move on to the last section—Release. This is where I would release my sister to the Lord. As I read, my heart softened toward my sister. When I said "Amen," I sighed a sigh of relief.

"Deanna, that was beautifully written, but it is very important to renounce all vows and lies spoken and believed about this event in your life." With that, she started listing out all the vows and lies I had relayed over our time together.

As I quickly took notes, I was shocked at what I had been choosing to believe about myself and my life, even in subtle forms. I then took a moment to reflect and collect my thoughts. I took a deep breath.

"Lord, please help me," I whispered to myself and then went on to renounce the lies and vows I had spoken over myself and/or chosen to believe about myself over the years. I renounced my promiscuousness, my drinking, the fact that I could act like two completely different people depending on who I was with, and my "fake it till you make it" attitude. I renounced my beliefs that I am ugly, I am a loser, and I can't trust men or women, and renounced my tendency to agree with the negative regarding myself. I acknowledged that what God says is truth, and not what **I** say, and He says I'm a princess. He says I am worthy of the love of a good man, so I renounced the lie that I am not. I renounced my need for control, evidenced by my decision to not date and to isolate and the lie that when people get to know me, they won't like me. I acknowledged that God wants good things for me and renounced the lie that God wants bad things to happen to me because I'm not worthy of good things. I acknowledged that this thought was agreeing with the enemy (Satan), as the cross paid the price of worthiness. I renounced that everything I touched was dark, ugly, and sinful, and asked God to forgive me for accepting deceit as my truth. And finally, I renounced the vow/lie of being a dream squelcher by assuming the trains in life are all going to hit. I asked for forgiveness due to my lack of trust in the Lord.

As I finished, the leaders prayed over me. Although I was again spent, this time I did not feel the need to rush out the door to be alone. Candace had told me to be vigilant— that God is faithful, and He will work in my life in this area. Later, as I walked out the door, I realized I believed her. And more importantly, I believed God. I knew something was going to change.

The days passed and moved into weeks. What I had at first believed to be too good to be true had become reality. The nightmares about my sister had stopped. I was so excited; I couldn't believe it. I decided to call my sister. I had no intention of telling her I had processed her; I just wanted to see how I felt as we spoke, to see if any of the old emotions came up. If they didn't, I would then know I was 100 percent healed. I nervously, but with great excitement, dialed her number.

My sister picked up the phone, and as I heard her voice, I realized there was nothing in my heart but happiness. I was elated! But I quickly realized I needed to talk to her about something besides saying "hi," and before I knew what my mouth was doing, I was telling her about Fresh Start and how much it was helping me. She was genuinely interested.

"Whom did you process?" she asked. And before I could check myself, I blurted out, "You!"

Oh, good grief! What had I just done? This was not the intent of my call at all! But before I could say another word, I was shocked by hers.

"I wasn't a very good sister to you. I'm sorry."

What? What had just happened? With that simple statement, I saw God showing up. I had given it all to God, and He was showing me what **He** could do if I just allowed Him.

"It's okay. It's all forgiven. I gave it all to God and it's done." I have never spoken happier words to my sister.

We went on to talk through how the process worked, and I encouraged her to look into going through it.

As I hung up the phone, I had never felt better. I didn't think but instead knew the relationship between my sister and myself had not only been healed but restored. I had experienced firsthand what God could do with one of my deepest hurts. And now I knew. His words from before resounded in my head: "*Do. The. Work.*" It was time. I knew I needed to process the rape. Would God really heal me from the rape? And what about the other nightmares? Would He heal me from the other traumas I had experienced? Would I be strong enough to let Him?

CHAPTER 8

You Get to Wear the Crown— You're a Princess

When you have experienced trauma, it can leave you in a place of negativity. In this place, it can be hard to see, much less believe in, the good. Believing it about the future and how it pertains to you can be very difficult. Believing it about yourself—impossible. This is where we have to let God come in. This is when we must remember that God is the author of doing the impossible. In Matthew 19:26, it says, "Jesus looked at them intently and said, 'Humanly speaking, it is impossible. But with God everything is possible.'"

The reality is that if we have accepted God as our personal Savior, we are adopted in as His children. This act in and of itself makes us princesses and princes of the King. So instead of believing the lies that Satan (our enemy), the world, and our own minds feed us about who we now are, we must believe God and how He defines us instead. In the beginning, this can be very hard, as many times we have believed for a very long time the lies of the enemy. We have taken on the identity handed to us via our trauma. Sometimes this ugly, self-demeaning victim identity can even become comfortable. After all, it doesn't challenge us to break out of our trauma prison. And even though the trauma prison sucks, it is a known place. The unknown can be very scary. Living in the "unknown" is where we first encountered trauma. The unknown is intimidating.

But the "unknown" is actually the land of the free! It is the place of unexpected blessings, the place of growth, the place where dreams can come true, the place where peace can be attained. Is it all rainbows and butterflies? Of course not. We will not experience that type of world until we are joined with Jesus in heaven. But I do believe it is a place where we get a glimpse of what heaven has in store for us— and it is indeed a beautiful sight.

The biggest hindrance to our breaking free from the grip of trauma has just three components: (1) not knowing Jesus, (2) not trusting God, and (3) not taking captive our thoughts. So how do we turn this around and break free once and for all?

Step 1: Knowing Jesus. Do you know Jesus as your personal Savior? I'm not talking about head knowledge of Him, because if you went to a private Christian/Catholic school, attended a Christian youth group or CCD, or even went to most churches, you are sure to have heard all about Him. But hearing about Him and knowing Him are two different things. I was raised going to church every week and went through grades 1–12 in Catholic schools. I defi- nitely knew about Jesus. But I never accepted Jesus as my personal Savior—as Lord of my life—until my midtwenties. Although I had heard about Him my whole life, I never realized He wanted an intimate, day-to-day relationship with me based on love, mercy, and grace, and not on my works trying to make myself good enough. I never realized that He was just waiting on me to choose Him. I never realized all it took was to say out loud a simple prayer (see below) and truly mean it in my heart:

> Dear Lord Jesus, I know that I am a sinner, and I ask for Your forgiveness. I believe You died for my sins and rose from the dead. I turn from my sins and invite You to come into my heart and life. I want to trust and follow You as my Lord and Savior. In Jesus' name, Amen.

The Bible says this about salvation:

> For by grace you have been saved through faith. And this is not your own doing; it is the gift of God, not a result of works so that no one may boast. (Ephesians 2:8–9 ESV)

> Because if you confess with your mouth that Jesus is Lord and believe in your heart that God raised Him from the dead, you will be saved. (Romans 10:9)

> He saved us, not because of works done by us in righteousness, but according to

His own mercy, by the washing of regen-
eration and renewal of the Holy Spirit.
(Titus 3:5)

And there is salvation in no one else, for
there is no other name under heaven given
among men by which we must be saved.
(Acts 4:12)

Jesus said to him, "I am the way, and the
truth, and the life. No one comes to the
Father except through me." (John 14:6)

I sincerely believe that it is impossible to be truly healed
and completely set free from trauma without a relationship
with Jesus Christ as your personal Savior.

Step 2: Trusting God. This is simple to say but hard
to do. For most people who have experienced trauma,
trust is a very guarded reward. Someone breaking a trust
is almost always a part of trauma, so instincts tell survivors
either not to trust at all or do so very sparingly. When I
first got saved, I liked to tell myself that I trusted God—it
was everyone else I distrusted! But after years of circling the
camp and not experiencing growth in my Christian life, I
finally realized that I truly hadn't been trusting God—not
with everything. When I finally asked Him to search my
heart and show me what was wrong, I realized that I had
kept Him somewhat at an arm's distance away. Yes, I had
been praying daily, reading my Bible, and going to church.
But the big things in life? Well, those were still being del-
egated to Deanna to handle. After all, I thought, God has

way bigger fish to fry than my finances, my dreams, and especially my feelings. **Wrong!**

Those, and more, are exactly what God is concerned with. He wants to be a part of every piece of your life. He wants to provide for us, guide us, comfort us, and be there for us in every matter—big or small. No, God having bigger fish to fry than my concerns was **not** the problem. The problem was that I didn't trust God enough to truly relinquish complete control of my life to His will. Deep down, I didn't truly believe He wanted good for me because I didn't believe I deserved it. After all, even if others didn't know, I knew all the inappropriate and bad things I had done over the course of my life and what had been done to me. Deep in my heart, I didn't believe I deserved anything good, so I couldn't believe God thought I did either. Therefore, subconsciously I had kept Him at arm's length, while still trying to make myself "good enough" for Him.

Herein lies the problem: We can never be "good enough." That is the whole purpose of the cross. Jesus did for us what we couldn't and can't do for ourselves. Now most Christians, like me, know this. But taking the head knowledge and getting it into your heart where it lives in your day-to-day life can be a whole different story. So it all boils down to trusting—stepping out in faith and believing that God means what He says and can be trusted to follow through. The Bible says this about trusting God:

> The Lord is my strength and my shield, in
> Him my heart trusts, and I am helped; my
> heart exults, and with my song I give thanks
> to Him. (Psalm 28:7)

And those who know Your name put their trust in You, for You, O Lord, have not forsaken those who seek you. (Psalm 9:10)

He is not afraid of bad news, his heart is firm trusting in the Lord. (Psalm 112:7)

You keep him in perfect peace whose mind is stayed on You because he trusts in You. (Isaiah 26:3)

Delight yourself in the Lord, and He will give you the desires of your heart. Commit your way to the Lord; trust in Him, and He will act. He will bring forth your righteousness as the light and your justice as the noonday. (Psalm 37:4–6)

Trust in the Lord with all your heart and do not lean on your own understanding. In all your ways acknowledge Him, and He will make straight your paths. (Proverbs 3:5–6)

The world says, "Fake it till you make it." But God says, "Trust Me and you will make it!" Trust is key.

Step 3: Taking Captive Your Thoughts. Oh boy—this step can be as challenging as Step 2 is difficult because much of our self-talk isn't true. Words have power, and the more we tell ourselves something, the more likely we will work subconsciously to make the message a reality even if the message is not the truth. Like most things in life, we do have a choice, even if it's not easy, to stop the flow of negative self-messages. This particular step was very hard for me. Here is an example: It has been prophesized over me more than once that I would remarry one day. My first marriage ended very traumatically for me. Most times when I heard this, I would laugh and say (sometimes out loud and sometimes in my mind), "Yeah, maybe in the geriatric ward!" That is a very negative thought. There is nothing in it that speaks of, or evokes trust in, the Lord or His time. But the more I said it and thought about it over the years, the more I believed it. The more I believed it, even though it was subconscious, the more my actions reinforced it. I found myself isolating more in my home and losing the desire to leave it. What you have to understand is that I **love** to go to new places and try new things. This shrinking violet was definitely not who I was or what God created me to be. It was what my repeated self-talk was programming me to be. My self-talk was teaching me that alone was safe. Alone equaled not getting hurt; people would hurt me.

As you read this, you can probably see the error in this reasoning. Can people hurt you? Absolutely. Do most people have an agenda to hurt you? Absolutely not. This is how the negative self-talk hooks you in. It typically includes a hint of truth that your traumatized self can relate to and attach to ("If I'm alone, people can't hurt me"), but it turns off your willingness to hold your thoughts to scrutiny. In this instance, scrutiny would have shown that all people don't want to hurt me, and I really don't want to be alone for the rest of my life. And the greatest scrutiny would be to ask, "Is this what God wants/asks of me? Does this line up with what He says in His Word?" In this case, the answer to both questions would be a big "No!"

When you take an objective look, you are probably starting to see how taking captive our thoughts is a very necessary step in healing trauma. But you also may be saying, "Great, Deanna, but I just don't know that I can do that." And I will tell you that I understand. I didn't know if I could either. By the time I started working on escaping my trauma prison, I had been in it for fifty years. I literally did not have memories of times I wasn't in it due to being traumatized as a small child. That's a lot of years of negative thoughts playing over and over in your mind. But I can't stress enough how important this step is: You have to commit to doing it. Also, realize that you won't be perfect when you start. If you are anything like me, you will often catch yourself having the exact thoughts you don't want to have! But that is why the step is taking captive your thoughts and not preventing negative thoughts. We are all human, so we will have moments where negativity seeps in. But this is just another place where God comes in. We have to reach out to **Him** and ask **Him** to help us take these thoughts captive to **His** truth and not ours. If we are committed and disciplined, we can become very good at immediately recognizing the negative thought, asking God to help us take it captive, and replacing the thought with either a positive one or a promise from God's Word. I promise you that the more you do this, the better you will become at doing it. It will start to become second nature. And with that, you will start to see the negative thoughts decrease. Remember, God is faithful and can be trusted to help in this endeavor.

A final note: Making the decision to break free from your trauma is very brave. Don't minimize it. Some of you are like me and have been living with your trauma for a very long time, especially if you have been re-traumatized by multiple traumas. As you walk this journey to freedom, be gentle with yourself as your heavenly Father is. Understand that although your Father is capable of instant healing, many times it ends up being a journey instead of instantaneous. Maybe this is because there is much to be learned in a journey? Only God can truly answer that, but I do believe the answer for many of us is, "Yes, it is." So when you are on your journey, surround yourself with other believers to hold you accountable (make sure they are strong enough and willing to have the hard conversations as needed); submerge yourself in God's Word (a version of the Bible you can read and understand so you know what it says); and, if led by the Lord, utilize Christian healing resources available to you.

A quick note on healing resources: It is very important to check these out and make sure they are of God and not man trying to use God's name to make money. Two resources that I can personally recommend are Fresh Start for all Nations (freshstartforallnations.org), which is free, and Gold Monarch Healing Center (goldmonarchhealingcenter.com), which is located in Abilene, Texas (there is a cost for this one). Although there are other good services out there, these are two I have personal experience with and am glad to endorse.

Finally, I want to exalt you. Breaking free from your trauma is possible. With God's help, you **can** do this. Freedom is powerful. It is a gift. It is a treasure worth working hard for, and it is worth fighting for. Trust God. Do the work, And You Shall Be Free!

* * * * *

Back in 2018

My voice caught in my throat. I couldn't believe I had actually done it. I had just shared with my leader, Candace, that I had been raped as a seventeen-year-old girl and needed to process it. I told her I had never shared this with anyone before, and she picked up immediately that this was a far deeper type of trauma than when I had processed my sister. She told me she needed to confer with the founders and would get back to me on how we would proceed. I just nodded my head in agreement. I hoped that when the time came, I would be able to speak my truth. In the thirty-seven years since it had happened, I hadn't been able to yet. When the time came, would I be able to now?

It worked out that Candace and one other leader were going to go through the process with me. A date had been set, and it was now time for me to prepare. I literally felt sick. Although I was alone with only my thoughts, I still didn't know if I could do this.

Good grief! I thought to myself. *If I can't do this alone, how am I ever going to be able to do this with them?* I picked up the *Fresh Start Processing the Issues of Your Heart* booklet. As I looked at it, I prayed, "Lord, help me get through just the first three steps, just this week's prep. I can't do this without You!" Having uttered that prayer, I steeled my heart to force myself to begin the task at hand.

Just like when I processed my sister, the first step has you identify the areas of offense, hurt, or loss in your life and who the offending person(s) is. To do this, I had to pry the lid off a jar I had mentally and emotionally sealed shut thirty-seven years prior. I took a big breath, and as I shakily exhaled, I picked up my pen and began to write.

> The offense/hurt/loss I am processing is the sexual grooming and rape of me by two cousins who were adult men. At the time, I was a very confused teenager who lived with a known alcoholic father who could be verbally abusive and/or violent when drunk. I was having problems with my sister at the same time. These relatives were very aware of all of this.

I then went on to explain in detail how I had been groomed by Relative A to believe that he was the only person who truly understood me. I wrote about how he used alcohol and marijuana to get me to this place, and how at one of his parties I proceeded to get very drunk, to the point that someone put me in the bathroom and propped me up against the toilet with my head on the seat, hoping my vomit would go in the toilet. I recalled in writing the blurry memories of trying so hard to hang onto that toilet while puking my guts out, and then someone dumping me in one of the bedrooms because I couldn't walk. I then described waking up from being passed out, still in a drunken state, with Relative B on top of me, raping me, and being too drunk to fight him off.

As I wrote down the specifics, the horror, confusion, and shame all came flooding back to me. The memory of waking up in the morning and not even knowing where my clothes were and how Relative B mocked me. How I had to act coy and make excuses in order for him to tell me what he did with my clothes, when the whole time I wanted to scream, puke, or just kill myself, all at the same time. The horror and shame I felt as I quickly dressed, with him watching, and then the anger that seethed in me as I heard him laughing when I ran out the door. The memories were so overwhelming that my hand shook as I wrote. Although I didn't want to, I forced myself to continue to write.

> As I drove myself home, all I could think was that I was a whore. Between the situation with Relative A and now Relative B forcing sex with me, I truly must be as nasty as my sister and everyone else thought. Later that week, I saw Relative A and told him I could not see him anymore because it was wrong. He never denied it and didn't bother me anymore. But Relative B was a different story. Any time there was a wedding, graduation, or family party, he would find a way to let whomever I had gone with know that they didn't have to worry, he would give me a ride home. Because he was a relative, everyone thought it was great. Because I hadn't told anyone, I couldn't say anything. He would smile that mocking smile

of his—that smile that said he was in control. He would try to get me drunk and then on the way home try to have sex with me. I was afraid to say no, so I would make excuses. I would say I had my period, he would say he didn't care, and I would say I did. This went on for about a year. During that time, I started to eat out of depression and gained weight. Finally, he must have gotten bored, or was no longer attracted to me because of the weight gain, or decided it wasn't worth his efforts, because he left me alone and then, finally, moved away. Unfortunately, people in my class at school had found out because the bedroom I was raped in was right by the room where the party was going on. I was told by a classmate in front of everybody in Chemistry class that I was disgusting. From that point on through graduation, I dropped in popularity and was pretty much ostracized from my class, feeling shunned.

As I put down my pen, I realized my face was wet from crying. But I still had two more steps to go before I could allow myself to quit.

In step two, you describe how you have been offended: what your thoughts have been in general and toward the person involved, including what your feelings have been. I paused in my writing. I knew from having processed my sister that for this to work, I had to be very honest here—

no matter the pain it caused me. As I put my pen back on the paper, I took a deep breath and ripped open Pandora's box.

My thoughts have been all over the place. Regarding Relative A: While I was young, I labeled myself as having serious mental problems. Who in their right mind starts to fall for their relative ten years older than them? But as I got older, I became disgusted. He should have known better. Why did he choose to groom me? I realized he acted like a child molester, and that made me sick. I couldn't stand him.

Regarding Relative B: I was very confused. I hated myself for allowing myself to get so drunk that this could happen to me. I felt like a whore. Relative B was good-looking, and deep down, a part of me was attracted to him. This repulsed me and made me believe I truly was no good. At times, I believed that maybe all I was good for was to be used by men. It wasn't until I got older that I realized that what he did to me was rape. Then I became angry. I was only seventeen! I should have been able to trust my own relatives! They should have been defending me, not harming me! But I had conflicting feelings and thoughts too. Was it my fault? Had I been dressing too sexy? Was I too flirtatious? Something must be wrong with me to have this happen. Things like this never happen to my sister. And then there was the boy in my Chemistry class. I hated him. How dare he announce my business to the whole class like he knew what happened?! How dare he act as if I was a willing participant? Who was he to judge me? I was so very angry with him. I hated him.

As I paused in writing, I noticed my tears had dried and the writing had become easier. Just as when I had lived it, I now had become very angry. I continued writing.

When I was in high school, this completely derailed me. While it was happening, everything was so out of control. Even though the time with Relative A was short, I felt serious shame and that I was dirty. And at first, I blamed myself for what Relative B did to me, and that made me feel dirty too. This was all so confusing to me, as I couldn't understand why this had happened. I felt I really must be dumb and stupid to get myself into this predicament. And then once the whole class knew, I was angry. When all my current friends rejected me and refused to hang around me anymore, I was lonely. I missed my huge group of friends! The rejection and abandonment were so hard! I didn't blame them for not wanting to be around me—I didn't like me either. Nobody wanted me.

As I got older, I realized that what both Relative A and Relative B had done to me was criminal. They were adults, and I was still a child! I realized how unprotected I was while they were supplying me with alcohol and pot. In high school, all of this made me sad and feel like an unclean loser. But as an adult, I felt rage and hate; I felt used and betrayed. Teenagers should not be victimized by their older adult relatives! And how dare the boy in my class judge me when he didn't even know what had really been done to me? He condemned me and marked me worthless in a public forum without even giving me an opportunity to tell my side. As a teenager, I felt trapped all the time by Relative B and fearful of what had happened and what people thought of me. But as an adult, I was angry and distrustful. Nobody was ever going to use me or hurt me like this again. I would never be this stupid again. I became resentful of happy people because deep down, I was jealous of their happiness as I fought depression. I didn't believe anyone would ever want me, and soon I lost all hope. I even found it difficult to dream. As time went on, I didn't allow myself to think about it. I had never told anyone in my family, and nobody ever questioned me. I continued to gain weight on and off as I struggled with depression, anxiety, and insecurity. And I just kept pushing it deeper and deeper down. The inferior feelings I had grew, and I learned to build walls to try to protect myself from getting hurt again.

There was no pause in the writing now. It was like the firehose had been turned on, and nothing was stopping the assault of words now flying from my pen. I moved on to the third step, where you describe how you have responded. This includes what you have said, done, and decided in response to what happened. I wrote about the boy in my class who had publicly shamed me and how he thought he was better than me, but I thought he was a judging ass. I wrote about Relative A and how he was a pathetic loser because normal adults don't hang out with minors having alcohol parties to make money off them, nor do they groom minor relative girls to be with them. He had some tragedies later in life, and I wrote how I never once felt bad for him because I felt as if he had gotten what he deserved. I moved on to writing about Relative B and described him as a slimy snake that I can't stand. I wrote that I hadn't seen him in thirty years and would be happy to never see him again. He raped me and led me to believe it was somehow my fault. I wondered how many other girls he had done this to. He disgusts me. Regarding myself, I continued to write:

> As for me—although I now see that I was a confused teenager who was taken advantage of, I still struggle. I struggle at times with wondering if my promiscuousness caused these things. I struggle with not being able to trust men—always wondering what they want from me. When I was married, sex was a confusing act for me. Was I an object to be used sexually in whatever manner he deemed desired/required? I never could trust that it truly was about love. I wondered if I was meant to be alone for the rest of my life because of this. I knew I shouldn't have been drinking or smoking pot at that party, but did that make it my fault?

I laid my pen down. I had done it. The pain, the anger, and shame—it was all there in black and white. But writing it down, as momentous of a task as it had been, was one thing. Speaking my truth out loud to others was a whole other level. I wondered if I would really be able to do it.

The week flew by quickly, and before I knew it, I found myself sitting down at a table with Candace and the other leader to begin my process. There weren't butterflies in my stomach; there were elephants trampling my insides!

As I walked through the first three steps of the process with these two leaders, I broke. After thirty-seven years, this was the very first time I had ever shared my ordeal with anyone. For thirty-seven years, I had blamed myself and lived under the shame of that blame. For thirty-seven years, I had labeled myself unworthy and locked my heart away. For thirty-seven years, without meaning to, I had sabotaged most of my relationships due to fear and mistrust. For thirty-seven years, I had yo-yoed, eating to push the pain and anger down, and then hating myself for the weight gain. For thirty-seven years, I had locked myself in my trauma prison and thrown away the key. And the bars on its windows and the steel in its doors were stronger than any physical prison could ever be.

As the session came to a close, I couldn't believe it. I had done it. I had actually shared everything that had happened! Not only had I shared the event, but I had shared my intense hatred for these relatives. This was a big deal—Christians aren't supposed to hate. But I was determined to keep this real. And this was my reality. This was my truth.

As I raised my eyes from the paper I had been reading, I steeled myself and prepared for the coming judgment. I silently prayed, "O Lord, I'm sorry I'm such a hypocrite!"

And then I saw it. There was no judgment in either leader's eyes. Instead, there was compassion, sorrow, empathy, and love. The type of love I imagine I would see if I were looking into the eyes of Jesus. I couldn't believe it! It broke the bars off the prison window I had been in, and for the first time in thirty-seven years, I felt fresh air flow over me.

As they prayed over me, encouraged me, and hugged me, they also cautioned me. They said the three final steps in the process that I needed to do to prepare for the next week could be the hardest. They told me to expect the enemy (Satan) to attack because he doesn't want me free from this trauma. "Lean in on God," they coached. "He is capable of handling all of your emotions and anything the enemy may throw at you."

As I got into my car to leave, I felt proud of how far I had come. But having already completed one healing process, I knew the toughest part was still to come.

A few days passed, and I knew it was time. I needed to complete the last three steps in the process for my next meeting. Although completing the first three steps was a **huge** breakthrough, I knew the healing and freedom actually happened with the completion of the entire process. It was time to sit down and complete the final steps.

I opened my Fresh Start booklet.

"Pour Out Your Heart"—I was to pour out my heart to the Lord, telling Him exactly how I felt, expressing my disappointment and current desires, and finally giving thanks to the Lord. This was the part I had been dreading. I truly didn't know how I was doing to do this, if I was even capable of doing this. So I did what I knew I could do—pray.

"Lord, I need your help here. I truly don't know if I can do this. But I do know You say **all** things are possible through You. **You** are going to have to carry me through this." I then picked up my pen and began to write.

> Lord, this is how I feel: I feel sad…so,
> so sad for the young woman who was so
> lost that the obvious was confusing to her.
> Why did so many bad things have to happen? Why did I have to be so beaten down

by the age of seventeen that all I felt I had to give was sexual? I feel like that girl was so tough on the outside but already broken into a million pieces on the inside. I feel sorry for that girl who was masquerading as a woman while really being a scared, lonely child inside. At the same time, I feel contempt for that girl that allowed everything to be taken away from her. Why did I ever fall for Relative A's words? Why did I have to choose alcohol and sex as my way to rebel? Where were my friends when I got so drunk that night? And why did I have to have relatives who wanted to use me sexually? It is all so gross—like a bad Lifetime movie. Where were You, Lord? Why couldn't I see You? I am angry, Lord. I am angry that I couldn't be saved from Relative A and Relative B. Where were the people who should have been protecting me? They were busy; either drinking themselves or busy judging and labeling me. And Lord, why did those two relatives seem to get away scot-free with what they did to me while my life went to hell? Lord, there are so many things I am upset about or wish would have happened. I wish I would have had a better relationship with my family so I could have run to them instead of away from them. I wish I would have picked friends who would have encouraged me not to drink instead of to drink. I wish that I wouldn't have been so insecure that I was gullible to fall for Relative A's words. I wish I wouldn't have fallen for Satan's lie that all I was good for was sex and that was the only way I would ever get a guy. I wish I wouldn't have been so flirtatious all the time. If I hadn't been, maybe I would have been braver to stand up for myself. I might have thought someone might believe me. I wish I would have been sober enough to scream when I woke up to Relative B on me. I wish I would have been sober enough and confident enough to fight back, scratch his eyes out, and kick him in the groin. I wish I would have been brave enough to do that and tell him off the subsequent times he came after me instead of just making excuses. I wish the boy at school would have come to me privately to ask me what had happened. I wish I would have been brave enough to tell him the truth. I wish he would have believed me. I wish I wouldn't have cut off my heart going forward. I don't remember after this ever having a completely honest relationship with a man again; I wish I could. I wish I could trust. I wish I could dream. I wish I could love. I don't want to be alone for the rest of my life. I don't know how to not be. Lord, I so desire to be whole, to have all the anger and bitterness removed, and to have the stronghold I have built around my heart removed. I so easily take everything said or done to me as an attempt to hurt or wound me. And I am tired of social events being so incredibly tiring. I want to trust people. I don't want to be socially awkward anymore due to my lack of trust or these walls. I don't want to push people away or isolate myself anymore. I want to be married again someday and not have the thought of making love to my husband make me feel ill. I desire a normal relationship that I don't try to control every part of. I want to treat my husband with respect and allow him to take care of me. Lord, mostly, I wish I would have never ended up so far away from You. I am so tired of taking care of myself. It is exhausting, and I want to stop.

As I paused, I reminded myself that in offering my suffering up as a sacrifice of thanksgiving, He would restore me. I saw it work with my sister, and I knew He could be trusted with this too.

Lord, I choose to give thanks for being in a family that was broken by alcohol and robbed me of my feelings of safety, security, and self-esteem. I choose to give thanks for Relative A taking advantage of this low self-esteem and grooming me to be with him. I choose to give thanks for the alcohol-laden parties I would go to. I choose to give thanks for getting so drunk that night and for Relative B raping me. I choose to give thanks for everyone finding out and that boy's announcement in class. I choose to give thanks for losing all my friends and status in the class. I choose to give thanks for all the promiscuous events that happened after this and the inability to have a right relationship with a man since. I choose to give thanks for the walls I have built and the lonely days I have had due to those walls. I choose to give thanks for all of the years alone and bitter. Lord, for all of these things I give thanks for, it is hard to be sincere. But I do it as a sacrifice to You out of obedience. I know You and only You can bring good out of all this. I know You understand better than anyone else what it feels like to be wounded, used, rejected, abandoned, unwanted, lonely, sad, betrayed, condemned, judged, victimized, and so much more, as all of this happened at the cross. So I give thanks that I can share in this with You and experience You turning bad into good—taking sins as red as blood and turning them into forgiveness as white as snow.

I paused in my writing. I had done it. By the grace of God, I had given thanks for what had happened. But I knew the next step would make choosing thankfulness seem like a walk in the park. The next step was all about forgiveness. I needed to forgive those who had hurt me. How in the world would I ever be able to do that? Alone, I couldn't. This is where God was going to have to carry me.

> Lord, I don't know how to do this. But I also didn't know how to be thankful for these things until **You** showed me that being thankful didn't necessarily mean being happy but instead can be an offering of sacrifice. **You** opened my eyes to see that the sacrifice allowed me to understand **Your** suffering at the cross more clearly, and that understanding allows me to identify with You more clearly than ever before. I need You to do the same work now in this journey to forgiveness.

I proceeded to read the Parable of the Unforgiving Servant. As I read, I could feel my eyes welling with tears and my heart softening under the weight of the realization of all I had been forgiven for over the years. I picked up my pen.

> Lord, I confess that not only have I never forgiven my relatives or classmate but I also have never forgiven myself. I haven't even tried. I took You right off the throne and put myself up there, holding the

scales of judgment. And when it came to me, I passed eternal judgment on myself that has lasted almost forty years. Lord, I am so sorry for removing you from your throne. I took one of Your princesses and persecuted her as Saul persecuted the Christians. I have replaced Your love and joy and instead embraced bitterness, judgment, and isolation. I confess that I chose a hard heart as though I was the only one who could protect me when, in reality, You are the only one with that power. By trying to take over and building all my different walls of protection—whether it be regarding my relatives, classmates, or myself—I was saying I could do this better than You, that I no longer trusted You had my best interest at heart and could take care of me and keep me safe better than myself. I confess a bitterness of heart that turned to hate for them and me.

Lord, I choose to forgive Relative A. I forgive him for hosting parties that encouraged me and so many teenagers to not only drink but also get drunk. I forgive him for supplying me with marijuana and encouraging me to get high. I am forgiving him for taking advantage of the knowledge he possessed of my broken home life and using it to do me harm. I am forgiving him for putting his physical wants over my mental needs by grooming me. I am forgiving him for molesting me physically, mentally, and emotionally.

Lord, I also choose to forgive Relative B. I forgive him for taking advantage of me when I was drunk and for raping me. I forgive him for having such a nonchalant attitude that next morning like I was a willing participant. I forgive him for smiling at me for the next year whenever he saw me like we had a special secret. I forgive him for seeking me out all those times and trying to pressure me to have sex with him. I forgive him for doing this to me in such a public place. I forgive him for always manipulating situations when we were in public at the same places to force me to be alone with him so he could try to get me to have sex. I forgive him for never once seeming sorry for what he did to me.

Lord, I forgive my classmate. I recognize that he, too, was a child. His mind must have been blown when he heard that I had been physical with my relatives. And I recognize that I don't know what version of the story he was told, but it most certainly wasn't the whole story and very likely didn't resemble the truth. As a teenage boy, this situation had to both disgust and embarrass him. I am choosing to forgive him for the public judgment and ostracizing I received from him at school. I am choosing to believe that he did the best he could as a teenage boy, with the knowledge he had. In a sense, he was a victim, too, and I choose to forgive him for any part in this.

Lord, finally, I come to the hardest part. I choose to forgive me. I forgive myself for seeking love in all the wrong places. I forgive myself for deciding to act flirtatiously and promiscuously. I forgive myself for always dancing along the lines of danger and going to Relative A's place where we could be alone. I forgive myself for looking for love in such a dark place, in such a dark way. I forgive myself for putting all blame on Relative A and not accepting my part in this. I forgive myself for not having more faith. I forgive myself for going to that party that night and deciding to drink so much and smoke that pot. I forgive myself for getting so drunk that I could no longer function. I forgive myself for putting myself in a situation where I could be raped with no effort— for making myself an easy target. I forgive myself for not confronting Relative B the next morning and defending myself. I forgive myself for acting like it was no big deal, and I could just go on with life. I forgive myself for the self-condemnation and judgments I made regarding myself following the rape. And I forgive myself for the hate and ill wishes I harbored for both my relatives. But it doesn't stop there, Lord. I forgive myself and recognize that I was a lost girl who may have looked womanly on the outside but was very young and wounded on the inside. I will forgive myself for damning that young girl to a life of self-abuse and isolation. I forgive myself for never letting that young girl off the hook and condemning her to a life of isolation, control, and self-hatred. And when that girl became a woman and gave her life to You, I forgive myself for stealing away her crown of royalty as heir to the King via self-condemnation. I forgive myself for choosing bitterness, judgment, control, isolation, and a hard heart over trusting You. I forgive myself for putting myself in a prison and throwing away the key. I forgive myself for all of the self-hatred. Lord, I choose to forgive everyone involved in all of this, all while knowing that it has stolen thirty-seven years of my life and very likely will require lots of hard work going forward to not fall into deeply entrenched habits of self-judgment and condemnation. Finally, I choose to forgive myself for not loving me as a child of

Yours, for You say I am a princess worth dying for. In Jesus' name, Amen.

As I lay down my pen, I realized I was so tired, just emotionally spent. But I knew I couldn't stop; I wasn't done yet. The final step called for me to release the offense and hurt to the Lord. That meant I needed to entrust the situation to God—to walk away from all the feelings, judgments, and thoughts, knowing God had much greater resources to deal with it all. It also meant I needed to, for the first time ever, pray for these people who had hurt me so intensely.

I sighed heavily as I picked up my pen. The fight was gone as my heart and soul were laid bare before my God.

Father God, I am entrusting Relative A and Relative B, my classmate, and myself and this whole situation to You. Heal all of us from these situations. I pray for Relative A, Relative B, and my classmate's salvation, acknowledging that I have no idea if any of them have gotten saved over the last thirty-seven years. I pray that if any of them are being held captive in their thoughts and/or hearts by the offenses they committed against me, that You would release them. Show them Your forgiveness and let them experience freedom in You. I pray, Lord, that You would fill me with not only forgiveness for them, but a love that makes no sense outside of You. Bless them with health and heal their bodies, minds, and souls. If any of them are held in bondage of any sort, I pray You would have mercy and rescue them. And finally, Lord, I pray for myself. I am removing myself from the throne—the throne only You should inhabit. I am putting my trust in You, knowing You love me and never wanted any of this to happen to me. You are trustworthy, so I can trust You to lead me. I pray that You will show me how to love myself—not in an idolizing way, but in a way that gives glory to You. I pray that You would take control of my heart and tear down the mighty fortress I have built around it; that You would instruct me how to be a woman of God and prepare me on how to be a godly wife for my husband one day. I entrust to You my future husband that even now You would begin preparing his heart to be able to not only handle but also embrace and love me—the whole package that includes my past—in a way that can only come from You. Lord, I pick up my crown and put it back on my head, as one of Your princesses. I entrust my life to You and ask You to guide me through it. In Jesus' name, Amen.

It was done. I closed my book and laid down my pen. All that was left was to verbalize all of it in my next meeting. I prayed I would have the strength.

The rest of the week went by quickly, and before I knew it, I found myself in my car pulling in to park for the meeting. As I walked in to meet with the leaders, I realized that although I was nervous, I was much calmer than the previous week. After some quick hellos, we sat down to get to the business at hand and opened in prayer. As I read aloud all I had written, the tears flowed freely. I couldn't believe the weight that was beginning to drop off my shoulders. As I finished, Candace spoke up.

"That was beautiful, Deanna. You need to know that you are fearfully and wonderfully made. He calls you 'Beloved'—you are the daughter of the Most High! But you need to realize that we can't forgive ourselves—only He has the ability to forgive. But we can choose whether to accept His forgiveness—as He is faithful to forgive if we but ask. You were made for relationship. I would like you to accept God's forgiveness and renounce all the self-judgments and vows you have made concerning these situations."

I took a deep breath. It was like a light had turned on in my head! Wow! I had totally never thought about that before. No wonder self-forgiveness never works because none of us has that ability! And Satan tries to convince us we need to be worthy to go before the throne to seek forgiveness from God, and between the two, he puts yet another lock on the door to our trauma prisons. Suddenly, it all made sense. The hateful feelings, negative thoughts, the isolation, the need to control—everything I thought and/or did to "protect" me and later my kids or to "punish" those who harmed me—

were all keys to more locks on my trauma prison door. I could hear the locks on my prison door starting to fall off, and I wanted to barge right on through it!

I then started to pray. I accepted His forgiveness and renounced all the judgments and vows in the name of Jesus. I renounced that no one cared and that I wasn't worthy of anyone's care, that I was good only for sex, and that sex was the only way to get a man. I renounced the decision that "if that's whom they say I am, then I will live the part." I sought and accepted forgiveness for believing the lies of the enemy that I had to keep everything a secret, and for building walls. I renounced the belief that I'm the token girl who gets the pity invite. I sought and accepted forgiveness for my pride and for believing the lie that something must be wrong with me—that I must be stupid to get myself into these predicaments. I renounced the vow that nobody was ever going to use or hurt me like this again, and sought and accepted forgiveness for saying I will never be this stupid again. I renounced the vow that I was going to control things because nobody was going to control me again. I sought and accepted forgiveness for being resentful and jealous of happy people and for stuffing my emotions by overeating. I renounced the self-judgment that I am unable to dream. I sought and accepted forgiveness for all the horrible thoughts I had and the labels I assigned to Relative A, Relative B, and my classmate. I renounced the vow that men are not able to be trusted. I renounced the vow that I was done—that I was just going to raise my kids and isolate myself to be alone because people were just going to hurt me, and I wasn't going to allow it. I sought and accepted forgiveness for my self-sabotaging behaviors. And finally,

I ended my prayer with these words: "Lord, help me to not take any of this back but instead give You the job of protecting me, including my reputation. In Jesus' name, Amen."

It was done. By the mercy and grace of God, I had processed my rape. I knew things were different. I felt like I was breathing fresh air for the first time in many years, but I didn't really know exactly what that meant. But I did know this: I felt free for the first time in thirty-seven years, and I was excited to find out.

Owning the Crown

As the car continued down the Texas highway, I reflected on the last few months. After processing my rape, I immediately had the opportunity to see what God had done. My high school class had our thirty-fifth reunion and, although I had typically not attended reunions in the past, I decided to go. I knew I would come face to face with The Classmate. As expected, I did. I was shocked (even though I shouldn't have been) to realize I no longer held any animosity toward him. God had healed that. I still struggled at the reunion somewhat, but I quickly realized that it was different. I found myself gravitating toward my friends that I had hung out with before the rape. For the first time, I had the overwhelming need to defend myself from the lies of the past. I only spoke with one person about it, but otherwise, I was able to refrain. I went to every event of that reunion to test what hold my past still had on me. With each event, I saw myself get stronger. By the end of the weekend, I had my answer—none. After that weekend, I realized something else: the horrible nightmares I had experienced for thirty-seven years had stopped. They were gone for good.

With two of the five nightmares that had plagued me for most of my life gone, I knew I held the keys that therapy had never been able to provide—complete release from the trauma prison I had lived in for so long. With that knowledge, I went forward and processed my son's suicide attempts. And just like with my sister and with the rape, my tormenting nightmares of the events around that stopped too. And the freedom I was experiencing was exhilarating.

Suddenly, I was jolted from my thoughts as the car came to a stop. I had arrived. Finally, I was at Gold Monarch Healing Center. As I stepped out of the car, a sense of awe overtook me. As my feet touched the ground, I had an intense feeling like I had never experienced before that I was on holy ground. The Spirit of God was so present I could barely breathe. At that moment, I knew that here, with God's help, mercy, and grace, I would tackle the last two nightmares: my childhood molestation and my ex-husband's infidelity. I knew that even after dealing with these last two traumas, there would eventually be more. We live in a fallen world where sin prevails, and man consistently falls short of God's perfect will for our lives. This means that we will eventually experience some degree of trauma again—some offense, hurt, and/or experience of loss during our lives. The difference was I now had the tools and knowledge to deal with whatever this life threw at me, with God's help, mercy, and grace.

As I walked toward the entrance of this beautiful place, once and for all, it was time to straighten my crown and own my inheritance. I threw back my shoulders and stood up tall. I was a princess—a child of the King. I could see total freedom at the top of one last hill and nothing—nothing was going to stop me now.

EPILOGUE

When I went to Gold Monarch Healing Center, I had two goals. First and foremost, it was to continue my healing journey and process my childhood molestations and my divorce. My secondary goal was to experience another format of biblical healing outside of Fresh Start to expand my tool belt. Prior to attending, I had done my homework, and I knew that Heartsync (Gold Monarch's biblical method of healing) met those criteria. My four days there did not disappoint. God showed up in every teaching, in every activity, in every meal, and in every session. It was truly an anointed healing time bathed in Him. Words of prophecy were spoken over me that I have since seen come to fruition. And when I left, I knew my world had changed. The remaining nightmares that had tormented me for years were gone. The horrific insomnia where I was lucky to get five hours of sleep was gone. Life was not perfect, as life on this fallen earth never will be, but life was good. I regained the ability to hope and to dream. The Lord restored me, and you can be restored too. No one is too far gone that they are out of His reach. Trauma unresolved, whether you are Christian or not, leaves you in a prison. After multiple unsuccessful tries with counseling/therapy, medicine, etc., I truly believe only the Lord holds the keys that can open the door and set you free forever. He has many resources at His disposal. I can fully endorse Fresh Start (freshstartforallnations.org) and Gold Monarch Healing Center (goldmonarchhealingcenter.com) because I have personally gone through their programs, but there are others. You just need to make sure they are biblically based and do not contradict the Bible.

Am I now perfect? No, nobody on this earth is. But I am whole and growing, and every day I get stronger. And by God's great mercy and grace, even through the ongoing trials of this world, I am able to continue to grow and strengthen. Yes, I have been restored. I am free.

HELP OPTIONS FOR THOSE EXPERIENCING TRAUMA AT THE HANDS OF OTHERS:

* National Domestic Violence Hotline—800-799-SAFE (2417)
* National Sexual Assault Hotline—800-656-HOPE (4673)
* National Teen Dating Abuse Hotline—866-331-9474
* StrongHearts Native Helpline—844-762-8483
* Department of Defense (DOD) Safe Helpline for Sexual Assault—877-995-5247
* National Human Trafficking Hotline—888-373-7888
* National Runaway Safeline—800-786-2929
* National Center for Missing and Exploited Children—800-843-5678
* Childhelp National Child Abuse Hotline—800-422-4453
* National Suicide Prevention Lifeline—800-273-8255
* Substance Abuse and Mental Health Services Administration—800-662-4357
* VictimConnect Hotline—855-484-2846

Did you enjoy *And You Shall Be Free*? Consider picking up the prequel to the story, *Grace and Peace* by Deanna Langworthy. Available in print and e-book.

SOURCES

Holy Bible, New Living Translation (NLT)[1]
Holy Bible, New American Standard Bible: 1995 Update (NASB1995)
Holy Bible, New King James Version (NKJV)
Holy Bible, New International Version (NIV)
Holy Bible, English Standard Version (ESV)
Processing Group—Statement of Understanding/Fresh Start for all Nations ©2013, Version 11.
Fresh Start It's Never Too Late—Processing the Issues of Your Heart ©2000 Fresh Start for all Nations.

---

[1] All Bible verses are taken from the NLT Bible unless otherwise cited.

ABOUT THE AUTHOR

And You Shall Be Free is Deanna Langworthy's second book, with her first being *Grace and Peace*. After having been set free from numerous traumas, Deanna is passionate about sharing the love of Christ with others while showing them the path to freedom. She is fully aware that it can be very easy as a Christian to fall into the trap of feeling as if you need to be perfect—saying the right things at the right times, never becoming angry, always being happy, and never questioning God. This isn't reality, however, and Deanna writes to show others that they not only can but should be real in their life walk and that they will find freedom and peace by walking in this reality with Jesus.

Deanna lives in Omaha, Nebraska, and is the mother of two sons and the grammy of three grandsons. In addition to being an author, Deanna is a public speaker who loves to guide others down the path to freedom and peace. She can be contacted regarding speaking engagements via her Facebook page titled Grace & Peace or by emailing her at Graceandpeace.dl@gmail.com.